Dr. C

Dr. C

Robert A. Rohm

MOODY PRESS
CHICAGO

The time line in Appendix A is reprinted by
permission of Paige Patterson.
"The Politics of Armageddon" is reprinted in part in
Appendix B by permission of Dick J. Reavis.

All Scripture quotations, unless noted otherwise,
are from the King James Version.

ISBN: 0-8024-1646-2

1 2 3 4 5 6 Printing/BC/Year 94 93 92 91 90

Printed in the United States of America

To my wife, Donna—
My faithful friend
and co-worker

CONTENTS

Acknowledgments

I want to thank my wife for being my faithful friend and co-worker throughout my graduate school and dissertation studies. She has typed, proofread, retyped, added, deleted, and made helpful suggestions throughout this project. Her price is "far above rubies" (Proverbs 31:10).

My four daughters have come to dislike the word "manuscript," but they still love their daddy. I am grateful for such a sweet group of girls. Each one is precious to me.

I want to express my gratitude to my mother, who went through some difficult days while I was in graduate school. The loss of her spouse (my father), along with physical problems, including surgery, did not stop her from always encouraging me to continue in academic pursuits as the years passed.

I want to express my sincere appreciation to my coworkers at First Baptist Church, Dallas, for encouraging me and giving me helpful tips along the way. Dr. Grace Wilson, librarian assistant, has a great memory for details.

A special word of thanks goes to Dr. D. Barry Lumsden, major professor of my doctoral studies. His writing expertise and helpful suggestions were greatly appreciated. His sense of humor is beyond compare.

My deep love and gratitude go to Sibyl Young for her financial support and words of encouragement. She is a special jewel in God's crown. What a profound impact she has had on me and my family!

I want to thank Mrs. Toxie White for long, tedious hours of tape transcription. She had listened to many of W. A. Criswell's selected sermons and copied them down word for word for me to review. What a labor of love! Also, a special word of thanks should go to Regan Smith for similar work done in tape transcription.

Finally, I want to thank my sixth grade teacher, Mrs. Dottie Bailey, for being the best English teacher in the world. She taught me to love grammar, literature, poetry, and writing even when I did not want to. I can still hear her now: "Robert Rohm, you are going to learn this if it kills you and me both!" It almost did. There aren't many teachers like her. God bless good school teachers.

Foreword

I can remember when I was a student at Southwestern Baptist Theological Seminary. On Sundays I would often drive over to Dallas from Fort Worth to attend the First Baptist Church. On one occasion I arrived early, walked down close to the front of the church, and sat in the second row. I wanted to have a good view. In a few minutes a rather large lady came down the aisle, looked at me, and said, "Young man, you'll have to move over. You are in my seat!" Well, I moved over! That story has stayed in my mind all these years. I learned firsthand that the members of First Baptist Church in Dallas loved their pastor and wanted to be "in place" to hear him every Sunday.

The service would begin, and from the side door in walked the pastor, Dr. W. A. Criswell. He stood up to preach and proclaim the Word of God. There was no compromise, no question, no denial. The Bible was the infallible, inerrant Word of God. His words burned in my heart. God's Word was truth. By knowing the truth, preaching the truth, and hearing the truth, he knew people would be set free.

There was always a response to the proclamation given. Lives were changed, souls were saved, and the church grew and grew. I felt in my heart God wanted me to join in the ranks with Dr. Criswell and other pastors who boldly and unashamedly stood for the truth. That was over 30 years ago. Not for one second have I ever regretted that decision. I have lived long enough to see the impact Dr. Criswell has had on many, many young preachers. What a role model for a young man.

Dr. Criswell will be loved, appreciated, and remembered by multitudes of people for many years to come. His life has counted for our Lord Jesus Christ. Because of his godly example literally hundreds of young preachers have followed in his steps. We are all proud of him. We are glad he gave dignity and honor to a position many of us love to be called . . . *pastor*.

God bless you, Dr. Criswell.

CHARLES STANLEY

Introduction

Almost every year during the Christmas season a classic movie is shown on television. "It's a Wonderful Life" is the story is a banker by the name of George Bailey (played by James Stewart), who experiences a frightening crisis. It seems that George's absent-minded Uncle Billy has accidentally misplaced several thousand dollars. Such a loss will cause George's shoestring bank to fail. George panics. He faces personal humiliation and ridicule, not to mention bankruptcy and charges of fraud.

George drives to the edge of town, walks onto the bridge, and looks into the icy waters. Thinking over his options he decides there is nothing left to do but commit suicide. Miraculously an angel, who looks like an ordinary man, is sent to help George. Clarence the angel jumps into the water to distract George. He screams for help. George realizes the seriousness of the situation and dives into the icy waters to save him. After they are both safe inside, Clarence reveals to a discouraged George Bailey that he is, in reality, an angel who had been sent to save him.

Naturally, George does not believe Clarence, and an argument ensues. George tries to end the whole discussion by telling Clarence it would have been better if he had never been born. George feels his life has been nothing but a failure, destined ultimately to end in disgrace and ruin.

Clarence sees his "golden opportunity." He grants George his wish. In an instant of time, Clarence creates an environment that shows George what life in his hometown of Bedford Falls would have been like had he never been born. Clarence takes George on a journey where he discovers to his horror that his brother Harry had drowned as a boy. George had not been there to save him. To make matters worse, all the men who had been saved in the war by Harry also died. Harry was not there to save them because George had not been alive to save Harry.

The local pharmacist has just been released from twenty years in prison for accidentally poisoning a child. In real life, George spared his employer that ordeal by catching the mistake. George's Uncle Billy (who caused this drastic situation in the first place) could have been spared a life of alcoholism and confinement to an institution by having a job provided in the Bailey Savings and Loan. But, since George had never existed, Uncle Billy had no one to help him. And rather than the town of Bedford Falls being a wholesome place to raise a family, it had become a run-down cesspool of "nightlife and immorality."

George begins to see how his life has touched so many others for the better. Finally he cannot stand it any longer. Although he faces financial ruin, disgrace, and jail, he decides life with a business failure is better than no life at all. He cries out to Clarence, "Get me back! Get me back! I want to live again!"

Suddenly he finds himself back on the bridge overlooking the icy waters. George realizes he has been given another chance to live. He runs home singing, skipping, and hugging everyone in sight. All of his problems have suddenly changed. George Bailey has a new perspective.

He had existed! He had really lived! When George arrives home his family and friends pour out love, affection, and financial help for all he has done for them in times past. He concludes, after all, "It's a wonderful life!"

So too the life of W. A. Criswell has made a difference. Without him, the changes in the educational philosophy of the First Baptist Church of Dallas, one of America's largest churches, would never have occurred. Dr. Criswell has been pastor of the historic First Baptist Church for more than forty-five years. Many of Dr. Criswell's education contributions have spread into the entire Southern Baptist denomination, America's largest Protestant religious body.

To portray Criswell's educational philosophy and discuss his contribution to the educational programming of the First Baptist Church of Dallas, we need to understand the climate of the church at the time Criswell came to be the new pastor. Criswell stepped into a difficult situation. He was only thirty-five years old at the time.

A review of Criswell's early life will also reveal some of the background influences that have molded his educational philosophy. Accurate history can only be repeated so many times before it becomes mundane. Dates, places, and events do not change, but their significance does. Next we will come to appreciate the significant events, contributions, institutions, and associations Criswell has provided or implemented. Conclusions will be drawn about the man, as well as the lasting effects of his influence.

Although Dr. Criswell has been the senior pastor of the First Baptist Church of Dallas for many years, this was by no means his introduction to the pastorate. In 1928 he was ordained as a seventeen-year-old minister of the gospel in Amarillo at the San Jacinto Baptist Church. That same year he pastored his first church at Devil's Bend, in Marlow, Texas. Later that year he began his second pastorate at Pecan Grove Baptist in Pulltight, Texas.

After graduation from Baylor University, he matriculated in the Southern Baptist Theological Seminary in Louisville, Kentucky, during which he continued to pastor churches. After seminary he pastored in Chickasha and Muskogee, Oklahoma. From Muskogee he came to Dallas. his pastoral experience totals more than sixty years.

By the early '40s, the First Baptist Church of Dallas had been catapulted into national prominence by its pastor, George W. Truett. At that time W. A. Criswell was virtually unknown. Today, however, Criswell is more famous than the church that once called him as pastor. What brought about this transformation? Those events and more will be discussed in this book.

In September 1944, the First Baptist Church of Dallas called Criswell to be their new pastor. Commenting on the difference between Truett and himself, Criswell often quotes one of the statements he overheard: "We have traded a gentle sunset for an atomic bomb!"

As a former staff member of First Baptist Church, and associate of Criswell, I had the opportunity to observe many of the results of Criswell's educational philosophies. One can read about Criswell and his accomplishments by the hour, yet miss the influence, power, and majesty of the man. He is a scholar of the highest order, yet he uses childlike simplicity when dealing with people. He is a fiery prophet, bold as a lion, yet he weeps compassionately for the souls of men. He is a denominational leader, yet he owes his soul to no man or denomination. But even great men have feet of clay and stumble along life's path. This aspect will also be noted.

Piles of books, paperwork, articles, and newsclippings are filled with interesting data about Criswell.

However, they could not be included in these pages. I believe it would have been easier to write on the history of the world than on W. A. Criswell. Therefore, this book examines one aspect of Criswell's life, namely his philosophical and educational contributions to the First Baptist Church of Dallas. Work regarding other aspects of Criswell's life and ministry contributions remains to be done.

I am indebted to the *Oral Memoirs of W. A. Criswell*, a program for oral history done by two professors (T. Charlton and R. Spain) from Baylor University. In quoting from this work, slight adjustments have been made due to the difference between the spoken word and the written word. But at no time has the meaning or intent been altered.

Dr. Criswell has had a profound impact on his twenty-seven thousand member congregation, on the church staff, on the school staff of Criswell College and First Baptist Academy, on the students in those schools, on the Southern Baptist denomination (both moderate and conservative factors), and also on the city of Dallas itself. He has been one of the key figures in the Fundamental and Evangelical national movements.

Presidents, Vice-presidents, Senators, and Governors have visited the large sanctuary in downtown Dallas. Dr. Criswell has also had an extensive ministry in preaching campaigns. He has been around the world on at least three occasions on preaching tours. He has preached to kings, headhunters, and little children.

Dr. Criswell is a significant person in the field of higher education. He earned his doctorate from Southern Baptist Seminary in Louisville and has been awarded honorary doctorates from Baylor University, Western Conservative Baptist Theological Seminary, California Baptist College, California Graduate School of Theology, and Hannibal-LaGrange College. He has founded two schools: Criswell College, and First Baptist Academy. He has been the president of the Southern Baptist Convention.He has written more than fifty books and has led many conferences and symposiums. He has composed many magazine articles and reference works and has been a regular contributor to Baptist publications.

Dr. Criswell has been listed in several *Who's Who*. He has been to Washington, D. C., for conferences of religious leaders and has been to the White house as the guest of several different presidents. Because of his life of service to education, Dr. Criswell and his pastoral career make a worthy topic for a book. As he nears the end of his pastoral ministry, the time seems appropriate to write one.

1
The Lord's Day

It is Sunday morning in Dallas. The time is 8:00 A.M. A black Mercedes is seen coming down St. Paul Street. The driver of the automobile (which was a gift from the church on his fortieth anniversary as pastor) is W. A. Criswell. He turns the car into the Veal garage and parks. One or two escorts meet him and walk with him to the pastor's prayer room. This room is located just outside the sanctuary. He joins two or three of the church staff, two or three laymen, and one or two guests. After the men cordially greet each other, they sit down and one by one offer a prayer. Dr. Criswell closes the prayer session, thanking God for the godly men and the prayers they have prayed for him.

The Early Service

One by one the men file out of the prayer room and head toward the sanctuary. Four men enter from one side of the sanctuary and four from the other, and make their way to the platform. It is time for the 8:15 service. The orchestra and choir are in place. The deacons, who will take up the offering, are on the first row. The sanctuary is full. The pastor has prepared his sermon. He is eager to preach. A Sunday morning at First Baptist

Church, Dallas, has begun.

One of the associate pastors steps up to the pulpit and says, "Good morning and welcome to the First Baptist Church of Dallas, Texas. We are so glad you are here today. Our deacons are coming forward to kneel at the altar, joining our pastor and the men on the platform as they kneel. Would you bow your hearts and heads as we go to the Lord in prayer?"

The deacons take a few steps forward and kneel at the altar. The pastor and the men on the platform kneel on their right knee. After this opening, songs are sung, announcements are given, and Criswell steps to the pulpit to read the Scriptures. Then the offering is taken, and one more song is sung. Criswell is now ready to preach.

As he steps into the pulpit one is reminded of a baseball player coming to the plate in the bottom of the ninth, ready and prepared to hit a home run. W. A. Criswell knows that God is in his heart (through prayer and study), in his hands (through the Word of God), and on his side (by being chief architect of the New Testament church).

Criswell begins his sermon. He preaches fervently and passionately, often weeping, throughout the message. As the service comes to a close, the invitation is given: "We want to invite you to come to the Lord. We want to invite you to put your faith in Christ, to join this dear church or be baptized. We are going to stand and sing a hymn of invitation. From the balcony down one of these stairwells, down one of these aisles on the lower floor, a family you, a couple you, or just one somebody you, come. And what a benediction it will be to your heart and ours. Come, come, come while we stand and while we sing."

Then Criswell will step down in front of the pulpit, along with several other staff members. Criswell will greet each one, usually inviting a family member to come stand by them along with a staff member. It is a beautiful time. Tears are often shed over the "harvest" that the Lord has given.

Sunday School

It is approximately 9:25. The first service is over. It is time for Sunday school, but the huge sanctuary does not empty. From 9:35 to 10:35, nationally known motivational speaker Zig Ziglar teaches the Auditorium Class. Zig Ziglar travels all over the United States and the world, but almost every Sunday of the year finds him in this auditorium. Those closest to Zig know that his Sunday school class means more to him than almost anything else in his life. Dozens of other classes are also in session elsewhere.

The Second Service

It is now 10:35. In the pastor's prayer room the men have begun to assemble again. Only this time it is a new group of men. The pastor is at the head of the table. Several of the staff are present, along with several laymen and a visitor or two. Sentence prayer is offered around the table once again, with the pastor closing the prayer time, asking God to go with them as they begin the second service. One gets the distinct impression that Dr. Criswell is about to go into battle. It is as though a war is taking place and the souls of the men are at stake.

Criswell is keenly aware that without God's help and the moving of the Holy Spirit nothing will happen. Jesus is magnified and glorified through the prayer time. One by one the men pray for the service and for their eighty-year-old pastor. As Criswell closes he thanks God for the godly prayers of the men who have come to "lift up his arms" and support him during his preaching time. One by one the men file out of the room and head toward the sanctuary.

Again, the orchestra and choir are in place. The television cameras are ready for the live broadcast to Dallas and the surrounding cities via satellite. The men file in one by one on either side of the auditorium. Criswell takes the first seat just behind the pulpit on the left-hand side facing the congregation. It is 10:50 A.M., time for the second service to begin.

The crowd is slightly larger than the earlier service. Many have remained from Zig Ziglar's Sunday school class. It is not uncommon for two to three hundred visitors to be present on any given Sunday morning. Most of the regular church members have made a faithful practice of attending the first service so that the visitors may have seats at the second service.

Excitement fills the air as Criswell steps to the pulpit in his white suit. (He wears a white suit each Sunday between Memorial Day and Labor Day. Then he wears darker suits for the fall and winter months.) "We welcome the uncounted throngs of you who share this hour by radio and by television. You are now a part of our dear First Baptist Church in beautiful downtown Dallas. This is the pastor welcoming you to our service." Either Criswell or one of his associates makes the preliminary remarks, and the second service is well on its way.

Soon, Criswell preaches the same sermon for the second time. Although television coverage stops at noon, the invitation lasts longer. By then, multitudes are streaming down the aisles, coming to be saved, to join the church, or to make another decision. After Criswell greets the people, loving each one in a personal way, it is time to go back to the parsonage on Swiss Avenue, eat lunch, and take a well-deserved Sunday afternoon nap.

Such is a typical Sunday in the life of W. A. Criswell. This routine, in one form or another, has been going on for more than four decades. Although some look at it as a "ritual," Criswell views it as doing things "decently and in order." It is his desire and goal for "a beautiful service to take place which will magnify the Lord." Churches all over the Southern Baptist Convention have adopted similar routines.

Criswell is the "godfather" of the Southern Baptist denomination. He has been called the Protestant Pope. But, as one gets to know him, he discovers that Criswell is simply a friend of the people and that he loves what he does for a living. In an assertion that rings true, he often maintains that he is just a country preacher who happens to be pastoring a big downtown church.

Where did this man come from? How did he get to be the way he is? In the following pages the story will unfold. As you read about the life of one of the greatest men of our era, consider the statement once made to D. L. Moody by Henry Varley: "The world has yet to see what God can do with and for and through and in a man who is fully and wholly consecrated to Jesus Christ." Moody's response to that statement was, "By God's grace, I'll be that man." Moody was that man in his generation. Perhaps W. A. Criswell has been that man in our own.

2
First Baptist Church, 1944

On July 7, 1944, then pastor of First Baptist Church, George W. Truett, died. His health had been failing since 1938. Until that time Truett's physical condition had been sturdy and durable. He was seventy-two years old when he faced his first real illness. By the fall of that year Truett was sent to south Texas for the winter to rest and recover. He did recuperate some, but by 1941 he was ill again. Two years later he was stricken with what proved to be his final ordeal. Although no official medical report was issued, those closest to Truett reported his illness as a cancerous condition in the bone of his left thigh.

In January 1944 a resolution was passed by the board of deacons permitting Truett a six month's leave of absence. No one wanted to think that Dr. Truett would soon die. Somehow they hoped he would escape that final appointment. Prayers and tears were offered on behalf of their beloved pastor of forty-seven years. Truett finally mustered the strength to stand one more time behind his pulpit and speak to his flock. That service is summarized by A. B. Tanco:

> I was present on that Sunday morning when Dr. Truett returned to his pulpit after an absence of three months

> during which he had undergone the operation from which he never recovered. On his previous appearance he appeared to be in the fullness of health. That morning, he walked in slowly with the aid of a cane . . . A noticeable hush . . . went over the vast congregation. It seemed stunned and shocked. . . . For the first time, they realized they were seeing the beginning of the end of the career of the great Pastor. Everyone seemed to want to express his feelings and appreciation in some way. Finally, someone timidly started to applaud and the entire congregation followed until there was a mighty applause. Of course the great Pastor never approved of applause at a worship service, but there was a difference here and he felt it as he responded with a glorious smile which came over his weary face. The invitation hymn that morning was "He Leadeth Me." I remember that, after singing a verse or two, the Pastor said "Sing that last verse," and then he went and quoted the entire verse. . . . It begins "And when my task on earth is done, When by Thy grace the victory's won, E'en death's cold wave I will not flee, Since God through Jordan leadeth me!" He and everyone else realized that his task on earth was done.[1]

In June Truett wanted to spare the church further uncertainty regarding what to do with their languishing situation. So he wrote his letter of resignation:

> If I know my own heart, my supreme concern, as your Pastor, has ever been for the highest spiritual welfare of the church, for her most useful ministry to our beloved city of Dallas, to our great country, and to the people of all the earth for whom our Savior died.
>
> I am, therefore, constrained herewith to tender you my resignation as Pastor of our blessed church. In taking this step, you will realize, I must believe, that I do this after weeks and even months of earnest prayer for Divine guidance, desiring only the highest welfare of our church. Her spiritual and missionary development has been, now for nearly forty-seven years, the dominant

> purpose of my life. Let me say that no words of mine can adequately convey to you the measure of gratitude of the Pastor and his family, for the never ceasing and overflowingly gracious consideration shown them by this church, through all the years.[2]

Naturally, the resignation was declined by both the deacons and the church body. Deacon Carr P. Collins said,

> The church has never before had to face an hour like this. I know the emotions that are in your hearts, because I feel the same emotion in my own heart. Many of us have never had another pastor. It is not necessary or proper for me to eulogize the pastor of this church, nor to pay tribute to him for the great service he has rendered to his fellow man—his life is already imprinted on the pages of the religious history of the world.
>
> While we deeply appreciate the noble purpose that prompted the Pastor to tender his resignation, it would be utterly unthinkable for the church to accept it. Anywhere in the world, when the name of George W. Truett is mentioned, the hearer thinks instinctively of the First Baptist Church in Dallas. Conversely, when one thinks of the First Baptist Church in Dallas, he instinctively thinks of its great pastor, Dr. George W. Truett. These names, the First Baptist Church in Dallas and Dr. George W. Truett are synonymous. How could anyone think of Dr. Truett except as pastor of the First Baptist Church in Dallas?[3]

Although the resignation was not accepted, the appointment of an associate pastor was recommended. On July 7, 1944, Dr. Truett died while still recognized as the pastor of the First Baptist Church of Dallas. The funeral was, to that time, perhaps the most widely attended event in Dallas history. Flags were lowered to half-mast. All county work stopped by order of the Commissioners Court to allow county employees to attend the funeral. The city came to a virtual standstill to pay tribute to Dr. Truett.

Although no one spoke of it, the question loomed: Who would take the place of George W. Truett? Who could fill his shoes? Who would carry on the work? Truett's years at First Baptist were great, but now they were over. Would the church languish and die? Had the glory departed with him? To whose shoulders would the mantle of leadership be passed? At that time no one knew. In a memorial service in Waco thirteen years earlier, Truett was quoted as saying, "God buries the workman, but the work goes on!" Now was the time to test that statement.

But the church remained in a state of shock. Truett was the only pastor most members of the church had ever known. There had never been a pulpit committee to search for a new pastor. Truett had become synonymous with the institution. It was unthinkable that anyone could take Truett's place. Yet a successor had to be found.

But what kind of man should be sought? A younger man with life, vigor, and vitality? A scholar who had prestigious credentials? An orator who, like Truett, could capture the listening ear of his audience? Could all these qualities be found in one individual? Most important to the congregation, who was *God's* choice?

The search began. Many prophets of despair predicted that the first man to follow Truett would fail. They felt the church would continually contrast the successor to Truett and "pick him apart." Prognostications were made concerning the congregation. People were beginning to move away from downtown Dallas into the suburbs. Only devotion to Truett had kept them loyal to the downtown church. Were the rumors true? Was the "golden age" over?

The Recommendation

The church in conference appointed a committee of seven people to bring before the church the man they recommended as the next pastor. The committee consisted of six deacons and Mrs. Earl Smith, who headed the Women's Missionary Union (WMU). The six deacons were F. M. Ryburn (Chairman), Orville Grover (Secretary), Chesley W. Brown, Ralph Baker, Robert H. Coleman, and Paul Danna.

Because of Truett's prolonged illness, the church had been in a position to host a long line of well-known preachers in recent months. "Among those who filled the pulpit in these early transitional days were such leading Baptist ministers as E. D. Head, W. R. White, Louie D. Newton, Duke McCall, Ellis A. Fuller, Ralph Herring, and many others. Several of these were considered potential pastors for the church."[4] But this decision was not to be made hastily. More candidates had to be reviewed.

The committee took recommendations from several sources. Dozens of unsolicited recommendations came in. There were thousands of preachers in the Southern Baptist Convention, and the committee felt it important to carefully review each candidate. After all, Truett had served faithfully for forty-seven years, and whoever followed him needed to be a man of noble character.

After a period of time the committee noticed that most of their recommendations had come from preachers. They decided to ask a layman for his opinion. This seemed to be a wise decision in view of the fact that many preachers "traded" recommendations with other preachers.

The most prominent layman they knew was John L. Hill of Broadman Press and the Baptist Sunday School Board in Nashville. Dr. Hill had preached as a layman from time to time for Dr. Truett at First Baptist Church. The people of the church knew him well. Hill traveled extensively; therefore, the committee felt he should know what was transpiring in the Southern Baptist Convention.

When the committee contacted Hill he responded quickly: "There is only one man in all the earth for you, and that is Dr. W. A. Criswell who is presently pastoring the First Baptist Church of Muskogee, Oklahoma."[5] Hill had met Criswell earlier in Kentucky and had only heard him preach once.

> How did it happen that Dr. Hill was so impressed with Criswell? As a student in Southern Baptist Theological Seminary in Louisville, young Criswell was pastor of a small church near Bowling Green, and he was present one day at the monthly associational workers' conference at a neighboring pastorless church. Dr. Hill and B. B. McKinney came up from Nashville to visit that meeting. Neither had ever heard of W. A. Criswell. While the men met in the vacant parsonage, the women met in the church on a cold, damp typical Kentucky "tobacco stripping" day.
>
> The leader arose before the small group and their prominent visitors and announced the program for the day had fallen through. Therefore, Brother Criswell would come and speak. It was the first the people had heard of it. It was also the first Brother Criswell had heard of it!
>
> No one could have blamed the youth had he declined to preach under such impromptu circumstances. But Wallie Amos Criswell was never the declining kind. With no advance notice, he simply arose and did the best he could. Afterward, Dr. Hill put his arm around Criswell's shoulder and said, "Young man, I've got my eye on you." And evidently he did. It was almost ten years later that Dr. Hill wrote so bluntly, "The man for you is W. A. Criswell."[6]

Evidently Hill was deeply moved by the young "fiery" preacher, but when the committee received Hill's letter they were amused. None on the committee had ever heard of Criswell. But they added his name to their list and continued the process. After several more weeks of work, the committee tried to narrow their choice to three names. The committee again turned to Hill for help. They called Hill and told him of their idea to narrow the choice to three individuals. Criswell was not included. Hill told them Criswell was still his choice to be their man.

The committee asked Dr. Hill when he had last heard Criswell preach. He replied, "As a student I heard him speak one time to a little handful of men at Smith's Grove, Kentucky."

The pulpit members were stunned. "Is that the only time you have ever heard him preach?"

Dr. Hill replied, "Yes."

The committee responded, "Well, what makes you so sure he is God's man for us?"

Dr. Hill replied, "I just know it. I am telling you the truth, he is God's man for this church."[7]

The committee respected Hill and decided the least they could do was invite Criswell to preach. One time would not hurt anything, and again, Hill's opinion carried significant influence with the committee members. Criswell was sent a letter explaining how fellow preachers had been trying to keep Dr. Truett's church alive in the final years of his illness. Now, since Truett was dead, preachers were continuing their kindness in preaching for the church. The committee realized they had come upon a unique way of reviewing preachers without coming right out and stating they were possible candidates. The committee asked Criswell to pick a Sunday in August to come and preach for them.

When the letter arrived, Criswell was in Ridgecrest, North Carolina, preaching at the Baptist Campgrounds. His wife, Betty, opened the letter. She called her husband and read it to him. Criswell responded, "Why, I will t do that. I will not go to a church that is pastorless and preach. I just don't do it, and I am not going to do it there."[8]

His wife explained that she felt this time the situation was different. "They have been preaching for Dr. Truett for a year and now that he is dead they are continuing to preach for him to keep the church alive. I think you ought to accept this time."

A reluctant Criswell said, "I will not do it."

"Well," she said, "I am going to accept it for you!"[9]

So Betty Criswell sent a telegram stating that the fourth Sunday in August her husband would be there to preach for them. Criswell noted, "When I got back to Muskogee there was not anything for me to do but to pack up and go to Dallas."[10]

The Dream

After Truett's death but before he was contacted by the church, Criswell had experienced an unusual dream. Because Criswell was not clairvoyant or overly mystical he did not think much about it. He simply accepted it as "just one of those things that happened to me."[11]

In the dream he was seated in the auditorium of the First Baptist Church in Dallas. (He had only been in the auditorium once in his life, and that was when he had been a student at Baylor sixteen years earlier. A Baptist Student Union convention was being held in Dallas, and Criswell had attended.) In the dream he entered the auditorium of the First Baptist Church with two men.

> "We sat in the bend of the horseshoe balcony on my right as I face it from the pulpit. The three of us went into the balcony and . . . sat down together. The church was jammed with people and the front of it was filled with flowers. In the center was a casket and the people

> were weeping, crying and sobbing everywhere." Then Criswell states that he asked, "Why are all these people crying?" The reply was made to him, "The great pastor is dead. Dr. Truett is dead." Criswell continues, "I sat there in that seat in the balcony looking at the great mass of people . . . and listening to the throngs of people in the auditorium crying. Suddenly the man on my right, who had entered the sanctuary with me, put his hand on my right knee and said, 'You must go down and preach for my people.' I turned and looked at the man and it was Dr. Truett. I said, 'Oh, sir, not I. I could never do that.' Then he put pressure on my knee again and said, 'Yes, yes, you must go down and preach to my people and remember to preach to them out of your heart.' " Then Criswell states he turned to Truett with tears in his own eyes and said, "Ambassador of God, I will give the best I have in my heart." Then the dream went away.[12]

Criswell did not tell anyone of the dream at the time.

Shortly thereafter another unusual situation occurred. Before Criswell was contacted by the committee, a close friend, Cornell Garner, stopped him and asked if he had been contacted by the First Baptist Church in Dallas. Criswell replied, "Why no, certainly not."

Years later Criswell asked Dr. Garner why he had asked him if he had been contacted by the church in Dallas. (Criswell thought perhaps Garner had talked to them about a possible recommendation.)

Garner replied, "I just knew they were going to do it. I knew you were going to be the next pastor of that church. I felt it from God." Garner further stated, "You know I started to write the Pulpit Committee of the First Baptist Church of Dallas and tell them to contact you, but I thought it would be a denial of the Spirit of God. I realized if God wants him there, God will do it!"[13]

As Criswell reflects back on these occurrences he

believes God was slowly opening the door for the transition to occur. Criswell believes God sends confirming signs whenever He wants a person to do something. It appeared to Criswell that these events were "confirming signs." Not only did a transition have to occur in the church, it had to occur in Criswell's heart as well. Criswell did not feel he would ever be offered the position because there were so many older ministers with more maturity who were already preaching there. Criswell was only thirty-five years old. Surely he was too young and inexperienced to be seriously considered.

The Trip

The end of August approached. As he boarded the MK&T train for the ride to Dallas, Criswell thought back over the years of his life and pondered the opportunity that now stood before him. He would give it his best (as he had promised Truett in the dream). When he stood in the pulpit to preach on that hot August morning he preached as fervently as he knew how. One member noted that Criswell almost tore his Bible to pieces, so fervently did he preach. The church, especially the pulpit committee, was more impressed with Criswell than anyone else they had heard up to that time. His presence demanded a sense of attention. The people in the church sat up and took notice as they had not done in months. There was something powerful in his presence and preaching.

> Criswell was a screamer. He did not reason with his congregation as Truett had done; he shouted sincerely at them. He did not stand straight in the pulpit as Truett had done. Criswell was restless, gesticulating and pacing back and forth as he spoke. Not all those who heard him liked him, but they did listen.[14]

Although Criswell was a younger man, he had all the qualities mentioned by several different people when

Truett had passed from the scene. Criswell had life, vigor, and vitality. His academic credentials included a Ph.D. degree from the seminary in Louisville. He was an orator who captured the ear of every audience to whom he spoke. He had several years of experience. And most important of all, the "hand of God" seemed to be upon him. W. A. Criswell became a serious candidate for the pastorate at First Baptist Church, Dallas.

After the message was over Criswell returned to Oklahoma. He felt that God had blessed him in the message and that he would be coming to Dallas. He also had his doubts, however, because there was so much maturity in the other candidates. Logically they would be offered the position ahead of him.

The committee decided that several representatives needed to travel to Muskogee, Oklahoma, in order to hear Criswell preach in his own pulpit. On September 17, 1944, three committee members—Ralph Baker, Chesley Brown, and Orville Grone—entered at different times and sat alone. They did not want to draw attention to their presence or put unnecessary pressure on the young pastor. As they observed that morning, the future call was taking shape:

> His sermon had more power than polish. At times his rich full voice was well-modulated, but again he might shout for emphasis and the clenched fist smashed again and again against the sturdy pulpit. A more earnest young man the committee had never heard. They talked together about him. They talked to many citizens of Muskogee, Baptist and non-Baptist, about him. They returned to Dallas convinced they should recommend him as the next pastor of the First Baptist Church.[15]

The Call

On Wednesday night, September 27, 1944, the church was called into an official conference. The committee report was read by Judge F. M. Ryburn: "We recommend that our church extend a call to Dr. W. A. Criswell to serve as pastor of this church."[16] Some discussion followed, including the idea that the committee recommend three men instead of one and allow the church to vote for one of the three. Then another unusual set of circumstances unfolded.

Mr. Carr Collins, president of the Fidelity Union Life Insurance Company and one of the leading deacons in the church, recalled a situation involving Criswell that had occurred years earlier. During the depression, Baylor University had launched the Greater Baylor Campaign of 1931, trying to raise $500,000 for the school. Criswell went to Collins and told him he wanted to help. Although Criswell only pastored two little country churches at the time, he had a love for Baylor, his alma mater, and wanted to do all he could to help them reach their goal. Mr. Collins was impressed with Criswell's drive and ambition.

When the campaign was about to be launched on the Baylor campus, Mr. Collins had laryngitis. Collins met with the president of Baylor, S. P. Brooks, and told him about Criswell. The two called for Criswell and explained the situation. They expressed unusual confidence in him. Criswell told them he would be glad to help and would do the best he could. The meeting had a long-lasting impact upon Criswell. The campaign was launched and was a tremendous success. Their confidence in Criswell would help shape his future.

Now that Criswell was being considered as the next pastor of First Baptist Church, these events began to return to the mind of Carr Collins. He stood up and told the church of his former dealings with Criswell and what had transpired. Many witnesses feel that it was his voice that carried the day. The committee's report was accepted by unanimous standing vote, and the call was extended to W. A. Criswell to become the next pastor of the First Baptist Church of Dallas.

The church archives list twenty-two names under active consideration by the committee at one time or another. The list included some of the most outstanding Baptist ministers in the nation. All the names were eventually marked out, except for the fifth name from the bottom: "W. A. Criswell."

After the meeting, Bob Coleman called Criswell and told him of the church's decision. Criswell and his wife prayed and wept together, seeking God's leadership to guide them in their decision. Criswell had held Truett's work in awe as the greatest ministry in the Christian world. But he wanted to be sure the church understood that he had to be himself.

> I can't be like Dr. Truett as much as I would like to be. I preach like a holy-roller. I know it and I can't help it. I have always spoken vigorously. I know that is a weakness. I have all my heart and soul in ministry and the Gospel. I am not proud that I sometimes shout and my voice cracks. I just get so interested and excited that I just can't help it.[17]

Criswell also informed the committee that he wanted full control of two areas: the pulpit and the staff. He would decide the content of his sermons, as well as who would preach if he should be absent, and he would have the final word as to the hiring and firing of church staff. The committee complied with these stipulations.

The first Sunday in October, Criswell returned to Dallas to preach in view of a call. Vivid memories of that service still exist in the minds of some of the older members:

> Bob Coleman started the service as usual, led the singing, made the announcements, and then introduced the pastor-elect and his wife. Criswell read the text from a New Testament with fine print. The heavy responsibil-

ity and awe of "George Truett's pulpit" began to weigh heavily upon him. His hands trembled so he could hardly see the text. It was noticeable to all. Paul Danna, who had not been very out-spoken before, said later that day, "Did you see his hands tremble? Did you see how reverently he handles the Word of God, not casually like some preachers? Yes, this is the man for us!"

At the conclusion of that sermon, Criswell knelt on the right side of the pulpit to pray for divine guidance. Others knelt to pray. Audible weeping broke out in the congregation. It was a deeply moving service. At the benediction, Bob Coleman took Criswell's arm and escorted him from the platform. Coleman (who had held out for another man) was unashamedly weeping. He said, "Young Pastor, when you come, and I have no doubt you will come for God has called you to come, always let the first Sunday in October be your anniversary Sunday rather than the date you move to Dallas. I have never before seen such a service.[18]

Acceptance

Criswell returned to Muskogee and sent the following telegram to Bob Coleman and the church:

> After these days of prayer, if all the membership of First Baptist Church Dallas still believes God has called me to be their pastor, that call is accepted in the name of Jesus. Let it be to us all a call of loyalty and love to our Saviour such as we have never known. Continue to pray without ceasing and to yield the leadership of the church to the Holy Spirit. We shall come to love and work with you the fifteenth of November, and now through the years may God bless us as Pastor and people. We love you already and pledge you the best of our lives. There is much to do. Let us do it with all our might in the strength of the Lord. (signed) W. A. Criswell.[19]

Criswell was now the new pastor, firmly in place. His first sermon would set the direction for his future ministry. The text was "There stood by me the angel of God saying 'Fear not'" (Acts 27:23). He decided to face the issue of being Truett's successor head on. He paid tribute to Truett but indicated that the church would not live in the past.

> Some of Job's comforters outside this church are saying that the man to follow Dr. Truett will be a miserable failure because the church was built around the incomparable personality with the silvery hair and the mellifluous voice. That the golden age of the church is over. That the church itself will die. Do you and I have the answer? We do! When I came to Dallas, Mrs. Truett prayed for me and said, "You will be as my son. My husband built the church not around himself but around Jesus Christ. And don't you be afraid of the task you have been called to assume."[20]

He also quoted Truett's own words: "God buries the workman, but the work goes on." Continuing, he said,

> We will go on and up with our various works. We'll give more to missions, more than ever before. We'll have a Sunday School with 5,000 in attendance every Sabbath morning. And the services in the church will be in the eye of God—not because of an eloquent tongue and a magnificent personality, but because of prayer, love, and labor.[21]

The new pastor faced his challenge and began his assignment. The historic church had been in decline, and there was much work ahead. If Criswell's confidence was any indicator of future success, a new day was about to dawn.

Notes

1. Leon McBeth, *The First Baptist Church of Dallas* (Grand Rapids: Zondervan, 1968), pp. 211-12.

2. R. DuCasse, *A History of the First Baptist Church, Dallas, Texas* (Master's thesis, Dallas Theological Seminary, 1964), 147.
3. Ibid., pp. 148-49.
4. McBeth, *The First Baptist Church of Dallas*, p. 220.
5. Ibid., p. 122.
6. Ibid., pp. 222-23.
7. T. Charlton and R. Spain, *Oral Memoirs of W. A. Criswell* (Waco, Tex.: Baylor U., 1973), p. 160.
8. Ibid., p. 157.
9. Ibid.
10. Ibid.
11. Ibid., p. 159.
12. Ibid.
13. Ibid., p. 160.
14. Dick Reavis, "The Politics of Armageddon," *Texas Monthly* (October 1984): 237.
15. McBeth, *The First Baptist Church of Dallas*, p. 225.
16. Ibid.
17. W. A. Criswell, *The Reminder* (a publication of First Baptist Church), 7 September 1956, p. 1.
18. McBeth, *The First Baptist Church of Dallas*, p. 226.
19. W. A. Criswell, *The Reminder*, 15 October 1944, p. 3.
20. W. A. Criswell, *The Reminder*, 19 November 1944, p. 1.
21. *Dallas Morning News*, 19 November 1944, p. 1.

3
The Man

The drive and determination of W. A. Criswell had their roots in his formative years. Certain facts regarding his family and personal background provide vital links to understanding the man and his mission.

The Early Years

Criswell was born on December 19, 1909, just east of the Texas Panhandle in Eldorado, Oklahoma. He was given no first or middle name, just the initials "W. A." Later he supplied these names from his father: "I just took it for granted in later life when I had to have some kind of name . . . because they had 'Junior' on that name . . . I just supposed I was Wallie Amos Criswell, Jr."[1]

His father, a widower, brought two girls and a boy into a new marriage with Anna Currie. Anna had been married previously as well. Her marriage had ended in divorce. She had two girls. Criswell states that as long as his mother lived she never mentioned the previous marriage or the fate of her first husband.[2] After W. A. Criswell, Sr., and Anna Currie married, they had two sons, W. A., Jr., and Currie. By this time the other children were grown and gone, so the only real sibling with whom Criswell associated was Currie.

When W. A. was five years old the family moved to Texline, a small community in the far northwestern corner of the Panhandle, a mile from the New Mexico border. Texline was mostly a railroad stop between Denver and Ft. Worth. Many in the community worked for the railroad. The elder Criswell received a piece of government land and tried to farm it, but times were hard. In an age before irrigation, many farms failed. The weather was harsh. Little W. A. failed the third grade in school due to absences associated with the severe weather conditions. So at a very young age W. A. Criswell learned by experience that failure was no pleasant event. He developed a sincere hate for failure at a young age. This would greatly impact his philosophy of life.

The government took the land back, and the Criswell family moved into the city. Criswell's father entered the town's commerce as a barber and for several years was also the owner of the town's only rentable bathtub, used by cowboys from nearby ranches.

There were two churches in Texline: a prosperous Methodist church and a poorer Baptist church. The Criswells attended the Baptist church. The elder Criswell was a devoted follower of J. Frank Norris, pastor of the First Baptist Church of Ft. Worth, Texas, who was also known as "the Tornado." But Anna Criswell was an admirer of George W. Truett, the Southern gentleman, who pastored the First Baptist Church of Dallas. Criswell still recalls the arguments his parents had over the controversial J. Frank Norris.

The Criswell family spent much time at church, enjoying evenings at church socials. When itinerant preachers and revivalists came to Texline, they often stayed in the Criswell home. During these times he would learn a great deal about Baptist life. This had a profound impression on young Criswell.

One Wednesday morning, W. A. asked permission

from his mother to be dismissed from school in order to attend the revival services. She agreed. The Reverend John Hicks, pastor of the First Baptist Church in Dalhart, Texas, was the preacher. He was also staying in the Criswell's home during the two-week revival. He and little W. A. had become good friends.

That morning when Brother Hicks finished his sermon W. A. turned to his mother. She was crying. She looked at her son and asked him if he would accept the Lord as his Savior. The young child began to weep and said, "Oh, Mother, yes!" He went down the aisle and was presented publicly by the pastor of the little Baptist congregation, L. S. Hill. He was baptized the following Sunday.

W. A. Criswell had been speaking all week with Brother Hicks about becoming a preacher himself one day. Now that he had been converted, the journey could begin. In thinking back over those days, Criswell reflects, "I knew God wanted me to be a preacher and I had the same conviction then I have now. I cannot remember when I was not going to be a preacher."[3] Criswell often makes the statement, "If I had a thousand lives to live, I would want to live every one of them as a pastor!"

Although Criswell's parents were elated that their son had become a Christian, they were sorely disappointed to hear of their son's desire to become a preacher. Though devout Baptists, the Criswells feared what the future would hold for their son should he go that route. Every preacher they had ever known was poorly educated, made little money, and was in constant danger of being fired. His parents hoped he would outgrow this childish fancy.

Criswell's father was once the chairman of a committee charged to dismiss a preacher. He told young W. A., "That was the saddest thing I ever did in my life. I would never do that again. If I live to be a million years old, I would never do that again. I will never allow myself to have any part in the firing of a preacher."[4] Criswell's father did not want his son to ever be part of such an experience. He gave the impression to W. A., "If you are going to be a preacher I hope you will be like Frank Norris."[5] It appears that Criswell's father had two mental images of a minister. One was of a lazy, undisciplined, sorry preacher. The other was of J. Frank Norris "the Tornado."

Norris was a colorful figure to say the least. When his church auditorium burned in January of 1912, Norris charged that his enemies were responsible. Following an investigation, the district attorney of Tarrant County accused Norris of committing arson in order to build a larger church. A grand jury agreed, and Norris was tried for perjury and arson in April 1912 but was acquitted.[6]

On July 17, 1926, a man who opposed Norris entered the second floor study of the First Baptist Church of Ft. Worth. D. E. Chipps had called earlier and threatened the pastor. When he arrived, sharp words were exchanged. Soon four shots rang out, and Chipps fell mortally wounded. A grand jury indicted Norris for murder. His attorney argued that Norris had shot in self-defense when a "stranger of unsavory reputation under the influence of alcohol provided apparent danger."[7] A jury in Austin tried the case. After only forty minutes of deliberation, Norris was found not guilty. Such was the kind of pastor W. A. Criswell, Sr., admired—one with power, control, and a sense of authority.

Criswell's mother, Anna, feared that her son would starve to death as a preacher. She had dreams of his becoming a physician like her own father. She even instructed him how to reply when asked what profession he would seek when grown. "I am going to be a doctor like my grandfather Currie."[8] Annie Currie did not want her son's life to be one of penury and want, always being unpaid and unsupported, with the possibility of being fired at any moment. At the same time, however, Annie Currie had great admiration for George W. Truett, perhaps the most famous preacher in the South.

Somewhere between the controversial and colorful J. Frank Norris and the dignified George W. Truett, W. A. Criswell would one day find his place. Truett and Norris were as different as day and night in their personalities, but both preached the Bible. Norris often preached on the "second coming of Christ." Truett, however, almost completely avoided the topic. Truett told close associates that he did not want to be identified with Norris. (For a full discussion of this topic, see Appendix B.)

As Criswell grew up, he developed an insatiable appetite for reading. His life centered on school and church.

> There was nothing in the community. There was not a picture show, we did not have a car to go any where, there was no radio, there was no television, there was not anything. I can well remember the first radio that I ever saw or heard. It was such a phenomenal thing. Well, the only thing that was open to me was to read. Practically everybody else was engrossed in doing something. They were punching cows or doing other things, but I had a tendency to stay at home and read. I read Zane Grey's novels, all of them that he wrote, and I read other Western novels, many, many, many of them. Then I would read all of those Horatio Alger stories and I would read the Bible, of course, and I would read the things that came into my hands that were given out by the church in its Sunday School literature and its Training Union literature and, of course, I studied my lessons for school.[9]

It is especially interesting to note Criswell's love for the Horatio Alger ("rags to riches") stories. "Those stories thrilled me to death. I identified with every one of those poor boys and I lived his life all the way up from the bottom to the top."[10] In time, Criswell would live out this experience in real life.

Criswell also borrowed books from his pastor in Texline, Brother Campbell. Most of these books were biographies of great men: Hannibal, Alexander the Great, Caesar, Napoleon, Aristotle, and others. These biographies would influence and shape the life of Criswell.

As a boy, Criswell attended every religious encampment that had a meeting: "I'd be right there, sitting in the class in theology, just a kid, say twelve years old, but when the preachers had their course in systematic theology, I was right in the middle of it. I was very much in it."[11]

Brother Campbell played an important role in Criswell's Christian growth. He took him to meetings that influenced him greatly in the direction of becoming a minister:

> When I was a boy Brother Campbell, who was pastor of the church at Texline, took me to an encampment that was just beginning in the Panhandle of Oklahoma—west of Guymon up there under the Black Mesa near Cimarron. And oh, those men spoke so encouragingly to me. They were amazed that I sat in the class of theology where just preachers were and I remember their talking about the questions I would ask and the discussions that I'd enter into. Of course, that's egotism for me even to think about that. But I remember it so vividly.[12]

Criswell was carefully protected as a child by his parents. His father would not allow a deck of cards in the house. Dancing was an evil, along with gambling and swearing. The home was very devout, built around the church.[13] Anna Criswell protected her son as well. She would not allow him to go swimming for fear he would drown, hunting for fear he might be shot, or to run around with other boys for fear he might pick up bad language. His life was consumed with church, home, and school activities.[14]

When Criswell was twelve years old the town of Texline held a tent revival. The guest preacher was Brother Whaley, pastor of the First Baptist Church of Memphis, Texas. At a morning service Whaley made an appeal for those who felt called to full-time Christian service. Criswell went down the aisle under that tent and publicly gave his life to be a preacher. In the same meeting an older man also "surrendered to preach." Everyone was deeply touched by the older man's decision, since he was already well into his years. Criswell recalls, "Everybody just thought it was so amazingly wonderful that this man would give his life to be a preacher. Of course, just a little boy such as I was, nobody paid any particular attention to me."[15] This slight would play an important role in Criswell's future dealings with children.

Criswell's Education

When Criswell was ready to enter high school, the high school in Texline was not accredited. Anna Criswell wanted her son to get a good education, so she decided to take her two sons and move to Amarillo. In Amarillo, Criswell developed a fondness for music. He played in three bands: the Hi-Y band, the Municipal Band of Amarillo, and the Amarillo High School Band. He also furthered his speaking skills by joining the debating club.

After speaking one time at the Rotary Club in Amarillo, a lawyer offered to send him to college and pay all his expenses if he would return and work for the firm in the summer and upon graduation. Criswell explained that his only concern was with becoming a preacher. The lawyer understood and encouraged Criswell: "You're giving your life to a greater calling and to a greater profession. God bless you in it."[16]

In Amarillo, Criswell's mother rented a house, then sub-rented rooms from their house to individuals. She took in sewing and baked pies to sell through the local drugstore to make additional money. Criswell's father remained in Texline. This family situation did not seem abnormal to Criswell because of his mother's strong desire for his success. "Whether it was for good or ill—my mother programmed everything for me. She had great ambition for me."[17]

A few years later, W. A. Criswell, Sr., moved to Amarillo to rejoin the family.

> It was just one of those seemingly normal things because my mother was so given to my education and to the preparing of me for this work that she wanted me to do. . . . It was just an accepted thing in the family such as your eating breakfast in the morning. It was just that normal.[18]

In a letter to one of the members of First Baptist Church in 1980, Criswell responded to the question, "What did your mother do to develop your life?"

> Several things in the life and care of my Mother for me greatly shaped every dream, vision and effort that I possessed in my young life. Let me list them one after another:
>
> 1. She loved me devotedly and devoutly, and I knew it from the days of my consciousness and through all the years that followed. To have someone love you is the richest possession in the earth.
>
> 2. Mother insisted that I get the finest education possible and available. That meant a doctor's degree, whether it was a doctor of medicine as was her father and she wished for me, or whether it was the highest degree in any other profession into which I might go. She saw to it that I went to school every day of my life.
>
> 3. My mother sacrificed constantly in order that I

> might have the finest training afforded in the barren country in which I grew up. By this I mean lessons in music, lessons in expression, lessons in public speaking, typewriter lessons and all kinds of things to help a boy grow in the use of his mind.
>
> 4. Most of all and above all, my Mother placed before me the image of Christ and the service due Him in the church, in personal life, and in all the energies to which we might devote every God-given talent to Him. There were no services at the church we did not attend. There were no efforts on the part of the church in which we did not share. The church was as much a vital part of our lives as breathing and sleeping and eating.
>
> 5. My mother always wanted me to excel. Second best was not good enough. She wanted me to be the best in whatever I was doing. That placed in my heart an insatiable imagination to succeed in the things that I felt God had called me to place heart and hand.[19]

Criswell's father had little influence on his son's education. In his later years, however, Criswell states that he came to appreciate his father and the sacrifices he made for him.[20] In Amarillo, Criswell excelled in school. In addition to being in the band and on the debating team, he made straight A's in his school work. His favorite subject was English. Still, his life almost entirely centered on the church.

On one occasion, George W. Truett came to Amarillo to hold a revival meeting. He also took up a special offering for the Baptist denomination. This had a profound influence upon Criswell. Shortly thereafter, at seventeen years of age, W. A. Criswell was licensed to preach by the First Baptist Church in Amarillo. Dr. G. L. Yates, pastor of the church, knew Criswell well and encouraged him greatly in the ministry. As Criswell's high school days came to an end, his mother visited several schools. She looked at each one and decided that her son should attend Baylor University.

Although W. A., Sr., had moved to Amarillo by this time, Anna was again pulling up roots and moving with her two sons to Waco. She felt it was important to help W. A. get started in college. She shut down all she was doing in Amarillo, moved to Waco, got a larger home, and started renting out rooms again. W. A.'s brother, Currie, was enrolled in the high school in Waco. Once settled in Waco, Criswell became active in the Seventh and James Street Baptist Church. There he entered into his first church role as the leader of the seventeen-year-old Training Union.

During Criswell's first year at Baylor, he prayed and asked God to help him make his way through school by preaching. He did not feel he was above menial labor, but he wanted to fully devote himself to the pastorate. By the beginning of his second year in school, his prayer had been answered. Once his mother saw that he was making his own way in life, she returned to Amarillo to be with W. A., Sr.

Criswell loved Baylor. He entered into academic life with fervor. Two professors would greatly influence his life: A. J. Armstrong and Henry Trantham. Dr. Armstrong was his English professor. Although Armstrong could be stern, he inspired Criswell greatly. He inculcated in Criswell a desire to excel, study, and preach. Criswell majored in English under Dr. Armstrong's supervision.

Dr. Armstrong played a significant role in Criswell's education. He taught Criswell by example that a man could be both intellectually astute and yet hold to the Christian faith. This impressed Criswell because of the public notion among those in academe that to believe the Bible and have faith in God was a sign of possible mental instability:

> Dr. Armstrong, even though he was . . . an authority in his field . . . helped me because he was a devout Chris-

> tian and I could see that in him. By this I'm saying, I could see that a man could be an intellectual and be at the very top of his field and still love Jesus, and still be a humble Christian man. Dr. Armstrong was that, and that encouraged me because as a young student it's easy to get all mixed up and bound up with philosophy and metaphysics and speculation and cross currents of theology and a million other things that you get introduced to in school. It's easy for a young man in the school to get to the conclusion that these fellows are devout because you don't have any sense. You're a Christian because you don't know any better. You love Jesus because you're provincial, you've closed your mind. Well, that's not so! And to see a wonderful professor who just is an excellent man in every way, and to see him at the same time devout and an humble follower of Christ, that does something to you. It did something to me.[21]

As time passed Criswell devoted himself to his studies. He knew he wanted to attend graduate school.

> One of the reasons that I wanted to go to Brown and to Yale was so many times I ran into the attitude that a preacher is an ignoramus, that he's not a learned man; he's not a man of parts, and that just always crushed me. I was so sensitive to that even as a youth, and I wanted to go to Brown and to Yale in order to show that a man who loved God and preached the gospel was not per se thereby an ignoramus, a man that didn't know any better.[22]

Armstrong was the faculty advisor for the Sigma Tau Delta fraternity, the most prestigious fraternity on campus. Members of the fraternity were selected by Dr. Armstrong. In Criswell's senior year he was elected president of the organization. Criswell admits he was fortunate to be one of Armstrong's "pets."[23]

Henry Trantham was Criswell's Greek teacher and another great influence in his life. Criswell took two years of Greek under him. The class had eight students and met in Trantham's home during the week. Dr. Trantham told Criswell that he was very smart and could understand things quickly. That encouraged Criswell to study and excel even more in school. Along with the encouragement that came from these important men in Criswell's life also came the feeling that there was little he could not do.

Criswell's Student Pastorates

During Criswell's freshman year he preached in many different settings to help him earn his way through school. One Sunday he was preaching in a Baptist church in Mount Calm, Texas. They liked him and invited him back. Thus, the first public response to Criswell's preaching occurred in Mount Calm. A young man came down the aisle, took Criswell's hand and said, "By this token [of a handshake], I am giving my life to be a Presbyterian preacher!"[24]

Criswell continued to preach in various churches. In a short time Marlow Baptist Church called him to be their pastor. The church was sixty miles from Waco. Criswell went to school during the week and traveled to Marlow every weekend to preach. He was only eighteen years old at the time.

While at Marlow something occurred that would forever shape Criswell's philosophy of education in church growth. Marlow Baptist Church was out from town a short distance. The Presbyterian church was in the center of the community and offered the only Sunday school program. Not being able to have a Sunday school of his own, Criswell began Sunday evening Training Union for young people. No other church offered an evening program. The strong emphasis on youth caused the Baptist Church to fill up. Then something unusual happened:

> I don't know whether this is very nice or not but this is what actually happened. The pastor of the Presbyterian Church, who was a tall, angular older man, asked me if we could go together and have a revival meeting. So I said, "That's fine." He said he'd preach one night and morning and then I'd preach one night and morning. We'd alternate through—I can't remember whether it was one week or two weeks—but anyway we held a revival meeting. Well, I had built up . . . the Training Union and got all of those youngsters and all those young people in the Training Union, so when we held our revival meeting *everybody* that came down that aisle joined our little Baptist Church and he never got a single member. Not one. Oh, it made me feel bad—I just felt so bad about that. But you can't help it. Well, the Presbyterian Church closed down because . . . when the young people and children came to our church—well, the fathers and mothers decided they would too.[25]

Criswell saw that the parents would follow their children to church if the children enjoyed it. This helped mold his philosophy of education and church growth.

By the end of Criswell's second year at Baylor, he had been called to pastor another small church at Pecan Grove. During these early days he held his first revival meeting at Pecan Grove. After the revival Criswell was told that no church of any consequence would ever call him to pastor because he preached so badly. That concerned him greatly. He sought help from an expression teacher.

After a few lessons she asked Criswell to preach her a sermon. Afterward she told him to return in a week and do likewise. Then she had a talk with him:

> She said, "Come here and sit down with me on this sofa." And we sat down in the living room. "You know, this week my dearest friend who lives in Kansas City came to see me and I asked her, 'Where do you go to church?' And she told me some such church. I asked

> her, 'Do you belong to that church?' She said, 'No.' I asked her, 'Why do you go to that church?' She said, 'Because that preacher gets up and preaches, and I like to hear a man when he stands up in the pulpit get up and preach. Just preach his whole heart out.' She said,
>
> "Now let me tell you, from now on and for the rest of your life when you stand up there in the pulpit you do just exactly as you feel like doing. If you feel like doubling up your fist—you double up your fist. If you feel like stomping on the floor—you stomp on the floor. If you feel like pounding that pulpit—you pound that pulpit. If you feel like shaking your head—you shake your head. You do just exactly as you feel like doing." And she said, "I'm not saying that people will like it, but I am telling you this—they will always listen to what you have to say." Now she said to me,"You go out that door and you don't have to come back anymore. This is your last lesson. But don't let anybody ever bother you the rest of your life. You be yourself and you preach just as you want to preach and I think God will bless you."[26]

From that time forward Criswell learned to be himself. This had a future impact on his philosophy of ministry.

Although Criswell was president of the Ministerial Association and active in Baylor life, his real interest was his country churches and furthering his preaching and speaking skills. During this time Criswell was called to pastor another small church in Mound, Texas. Mound and Pecan Grove were only a few miles apart. Therefore, Criswell resigned his church in Marlow and began to alternate Sundays between Mound and Pecan Grove.

In May 1931, Criswell's years at Baylor came to an end. He graduated "with high honors," majoring in English. It is worth mentioning that Criswell's educational experience placed heavy doubts in his heart regarding his Christian faith. He minored in psychology and philosophy. Being inquisitive by nature, Criswell sought an answer for every question. Sometimes he was left with intellectual doubts. He learned to stay balanced, however, by keeping in close touch with the realities of daily life and with the pain of human suffering.

> The best thing to do is to stay around people. This is very apparent in the life of any minister. I don't care how intellectually he may get all wound up . . . when you get down to the needs of people, we're all fundamentally leaning on God, I mean there's no other answer. Here is death, the death of a child, or here is a catastrophic accident that has happened and just brings with it indescribable heartache and suffering. Well, when you're down there working with people, your intellectual doubts . . . are just not pertinent. They are things to discuss, but when you're down here where the people are, trying to minister to them, you just move into another world. There it's either God or nothing. You're faced with either a trust in the goodness and the mercy of the Lord or just being a blank infidel.[27]

After graduation he decided to broaden his horizons, move out of the state, and attend the Southern Baptist Seminary in Louisville, Kentucky. Criswell had a friend attending Yale University who wanted him to attend there as well. A Quaker church in Rhode Island was ready to call Criswell as pastor. Criswell was advised that Yale would prepare him for a position as a professor in a university. If he wanted to be a pastor, however, he was advised to attend Southern Seminary. So the decision, in the final analysis, was an easy one.

When Criswell arrived in Kentucky he knew the route he must travel. He would work his way through school by pastoring churches. Criswell and a friend attended Baptist associational meetings, and both received many invitations to preach at pastorless churches. The Depression had begun, and many of the smaller churches could not afford to have a full-time pastor. Criswell accepted the call to pastor at Mount Washington, seven miles from Louisville. He would be there three Sundays each month. Another church, much farther away in Oakland, Kentucky, ten miles northeast of Bowling Green, called him as pastor on a one time per month basis. So again, Criswell was ready to begin his education endeavors with his financial commitments in order.

Criswell prepared to begin his graduate work under the famed A. T. Robertson. Many believe Robertson was the greatest Southern Baptist scholar who ever lived. Criswell studied under him for three years, completing his master's degree. Criswell then began his doctoral work, again, under Robertson's supervision. In the first month of study, however, Dr. Robertson died. Hersey Davis, Robertson's associate, took his place. Davis had a profound influence upon Criswell. Robertson was a stern man, whereas Dr. Davis was more kindly. By his example he would impact Criswell and his educational philosophy.

Criswell continued to excel in New Testament Greek, in which he majored. Old Testament Hebrew was more difficult for him, largely due to time constraints. Keeping up with two churches left little time to study the Hebrew language. Also, by this time Criswell was getting older, maturing, and becoming more interested in entering his life's work as a full-time pastor rather than simply being a student.

Criswell had a double minor in seminary: one in theology and the other in contemporary social movements. He rejects the notion that he is uninterested in societal needs:

> The reading of history and modern revolutionary movements have brought us to our present hour. Fascism, Naziism, socialism, communism finally plunged the whole earth into war. Well, those things just violently interested me.[28]

A book entitled *The Social Conscience of W. A. Criswell*[29] goes into detail regarding Criswell's fondness for social interaction. Patterson notes, however, that the book did not sell well because it was not marketed well.[30]

No one charges Criswell with being "so heavenly minded that he is no earthly good." He stays involved in daily activities that interest most people. There is even a joke about Criswell that circulates: When Criswell got to heaven, St. Peter could not locate his name in God's book. Finally, after a few minutes, Peter found it. It was listed under "real estate." Perhaps one of the reasons the people of First Baptist Church respect their pastor so much is because of his keen business mind:

> Some men are interested in fishing, hunting, golf. But the investment world enthralls me and God has blessed me in it. God gave me a knack for making money but I don't have much time to dedicate to it—yet I'm not a poor man.[31]

After completing his master's degree in 1934, he remained at Southern Seminary for doctoral work. Criswell met a young schoolteacher, Betty Harris, who was the church pianist at Mount Washington. He desired to court her, yet felt it wrong since she was a member of his church. He resigned and took another church pastorate in Woodburn, some twenty miles south of Bowling Green. He began alternating Sundays between Oakland and Woodburn.

On Valentine's Day, February 14, 1935, Criswell married Betty Marie Harris. They lived in Bowling Green because it was centrally located to all their activities. Whether or not getting married on Valentine's Day is a flair for the dramatic remains unknown. One thing is true, however: this is simply another example of how Criswell tried to accomplish his tasks in the best manner possible.

Criswell continued to pastor these two churches and pursue his degree. His dissertation was entitled "The John the Baptist Movement in Relation to the Christian Movement." In May 1937 he was awarded the Ph.D. degree by the Southern Baptist Theological Seminary in Louisville.

PASTORING IN CHICKASHA

After graduation, W. A. and his wife did not know which direction to pursue. They prayed together and told God they would take the first church that called Criswell as full-time pastor. They further agreed to tell no one of their secret decision.

The First Baptist Church of Birmingham, Alabama, invited Criswell to come preach. The pastor of the church, J. R. Hobbs, had become incapacitated because of a heart attack. John L. Hill had recommended Criswell to Dr. Hobbs. Criswell preached at the church, and Dr. Hobbs listened over the radio. Afterward Criswell was taken to meet Dr. Hobbs. He was delighted with Criswell and told him he wanted him to be pastor of the church. Hill talked to the pulpit committee, and everything seemed to be in order. It appeared Criswell would soon be called as the next pastor of the First Baptist Church of Birmingham, Alabama.

A few weeks passed. The doctors delayed in making their final report on Dr. Hobbs. Everyone hoped he would get better. The report was finally made that Dr. Hobbs could not be pastor of the church any longer. In the meantime the First Baptist Church of Chickasha, Oklahoma, called Criswell to be their new pastor.

Some of the people at Chickasha heard Criswell at a Bible conference in Ridgecrest, North Carolina. When their pastor, J. W. Bruner, resigned to move to Texas, Criswell was their first choice. The first official call had come. Two weeks later, however, the call came from the

First Baptist Church in Birmingham, Alabama, a much larger and more prestigious church. But W. A. and Betty Criswell had made a promise to God. They accepted the position in Chickasha.

Hill, somewhat disturbed, contacted Criswell. Criswell revealed the covenant he and his wife had earlier made with God. Hill concurred that, if he had that conviction in his heart, he should go.

The church in Chickasha had a membership of about two thousand. It was a nice church, by far the largest and most influential church in the city. When Criswell arrived, the church began to grow immediately. Under his leadership the church built a large tabernacle. This became a pattern Criswell followed: namely, getting a building program underway at the outset of his pastorate.

> There was a man, a very fine businessman in Chickasha, who came to visit the church. He had to stand in the door. There was no room nor seat for him, so he stood in the door and listened to me preach. After it was over he came up to me and said, "Young man, let me tell you, the preacher that can fill a church like this in Chickasha can fill the biggest auditorium in the land." Oh, I remember that so well.[32]

Criswell's reputation began to spread. He was invited to be active in Southern Baptist denominational work. He was placed on the Executive Board for the state of Oklahoma, as well as on the Board of Trustees for Oklahoma Baptist University. He was asked to preach the state convention sermon his first year in Oklahoma. This was an honor many preachers hoped for in a lifetime. Criswell was only twenty-seven years old at the time.

Something was different about Criswell, and people noticed it. Here was a well-educated man with a Ph.D.

degree who preached like a "holy roller," a label that began to characterize him and his abilities. Criswell remained in Chickasha from 1937 to 1941.

Pastoring in Muskogee

In December 1940 A. N. Hall, pastor of the First Baptist church of Muskogee, Oklahoma, died. He and Criswell had been friends. Criswell once visited the church in Muskogee and spoke at a banquet. Dr. Hall, an older man, was about seventy-five years old at that time. Dr. Hall told some of his church leaders in Muskogee that if anything ever happened to him, he wanted them to call Criswell as his successor.

Dr. Hall was getting dressed one Sunday morning, preparing to go to church. Suddenly he was stricken ill and died. On his desk was the outline for his sermon: "My First Five Minutes in Heaven." That was now a reality. The pulpit committee was appointed the second Sunday in January 1941. At 1:00 in the afternoon, Criswell was called to be their next pastor. After prayer and consideration, W. A., Betty, and their two-year-old daughter, Mabel Anne, moved to Muskogee.

The Criswells, especially Betty, loved Muskogee. God blessed them in their work, and the church grew. Immediately Criswell led the church in renovating an old building and converting it into an educational facility.

While at Muskogee an interesting shift occurred in Criswell's preaching. Until now he had been a topical preacher, preaching on different subjects each sermon. Now he began to preach through sections of the Bible. Criswell says that it may have been the result of looking through Dr. Hall's personal library, given to him by Hall's wife.

> It would be difficult for me to describe how much of a different world it was for me. I was fascinated by what

> I was doing. Instead of sermons coming laboriously and pacing the floor on Monday or Tuesday, wondering what in the world am I going to preach about the following Sunday, now there was so much to say and so many things to learn and to preach about that I was not going to have the length of days in which to do it. Where I left off one Sunday I would start the next.[33]

The church in Muskogee flourished under Criswell's leadership. Another building program was under way, and Criswell's career was expanding. For summer vacation Criswell would go on preaching tours, while his wife and daughter visited relatives in Kentucky. In August of 1944 Criswell went to Ridgecrest, North Carolina, to preach at the Baptist Campgrounds. From there he went to St. Petersburg, Florida, for another speaking engagement.

One month earlier, George W. Truett died. The whole Baptist world mourned his death. Truett was in a class by himself. No one could take his place. But the church had to go on. The full details of these events were explained in chapter 2. On September 27, 1944, Criswell was called to be the new pastor of the First Baptist Church of Dallas, Texas. A new day had come.

Notes

1. T. Charlton and R. Spain, *Oral Memoirs of W. A. Criswell* (Waco, Tex.: Baylor Univ., 1973), p. 3.
2. Dick Reavis, "The Politics of Armageddon," *Texas Monthly* (October 1984): 235-36.
3. B. Keith, *W. A. Criswell: The Authorized Biography* (Old Tappan, N. J.: Revell, 1973), p. 21.
4. Charlton and Spain, *Oral Memoirs*, p. 20.
5. Ibid., p. 22.
6. C. Allyn Russell, *Voices of American Fundamentalism: Seven Biographical Studies* (Philadelphia: Westminster, 1976), p. 34.
7. Ibid.
8. Charlton and Spain, *Oral Memoirs*, p. 3.
9. Ibid., p.13.

10. Ibid., p. 15.
11. Ibid., p. 34.
12. Ibid., pp. 56-57.
13. Ibid., p. 28.
14. Ibid., p. 39.
15. Ibid., p. 30.
17. Ibid., p. 43.
18. Ibid., p. 44.
19. W. A. Criswell, personal communication, 5 June 1980.
20. Charlton and Spain, *Oral Memoirs*, p. 46.
21. Ibid., pp. 110-11.
22. Ibid., p. 120.
23. Ibid., p. 102.
24. W. A. Criswell, *The Reminder* (a publication of First Baptist Church), 14 July 1946, p. 1.
25. Ibid., p. 70.
26. Ibid., pp. 74-75.
27. Ibid., pp. 108-9.
28. Ibid., p. 138.
29. J. E. Towns, *The Social Conscience of W. A. Criswell* (Dallas: Crescendo, 1977).
30. P. Patterson, "The Imponderables of God," *Criswell Theological Review* 1, no. 2:25.
31. Keith, *W. A. Criswell*, p. 137.
32. Charlton and Spain, *Oral Memoirs*, p. 150.
33. Ibid., p. 162.

4
The Move

For the third time in Criswell's brief career he had been called to follow an older man. In Chickasha he followed J. W. Bruner, who had pastored there for fifteen years. In Muskogee he followed A. N. Hall upon his death. Dr. Hall had been pastor in Muskogee for twenty-eight years. Now Criswell was called to follow Dr. Truett, who had pastored the First Baptist Church of Dallas for forty-seven years and was Criswell's senior by more than forty years. Criswell's experience in those two earlier pastorates helped him immensely.

The Criswells moved into their present home on Swiss Avenue in Dallas. The church purchased the parsonage for $15,500. The home has appreciated in value over the years manyfold. Now the value is in the neighborhood of half a million dollars.

Criswell, humbly but firmly, assumed the responsibilities of leadership of the First Baptist Church in October 1944. Although there were a few families who left the church, not tolerating anyone who would follow Dr. Truett, there was no significant decrease in membership.

> I would suppose that there were some people who resented anybody following Dr. Truett. In fact, one family

> that very poignantly brought sorrow to my heart left on that account because I was the successor of Dr. Truett, but that was the rare exception. The vast, vast body of the church received me as God's man to follow Dr. Truett. And the same affection by which they always referred to Dr. Truett as "Pastor" immediately, though I was so much younger, they used that same word in the same affection to refer to me. I was always, "Pastor."[1]

The church began to receive new members immediately. No obstacle was too large to overcome in Criswell's eyes. He was convinced that God was directing him, as He always had, to preach the gospel to all who would come and hear. Criswell felt that it was his responsibility to see that they did come. He knew the kind of church he wanted to build but had not yet formulated a specific program to build it.

Criswell spent the first year getting acquainted with the church and winning the full confidence of his people. During this transition period he focused on the pulpit ministry with dynamic preaching. Criswell has often noted that his first impression of the church as he began his ministry was that of "wood." The pews were made of wood, as were the banister, railings, and panels. The crowds were not present to occupy the pews, therefore a lot wood of could be seen. Criswell was not interested in looking at wood. He wanted to see people. As the reputation of this fiery young preacher spread, the church began to grow.

Bob Coleman, who had been Dr. Truett's right-hand man, was of tremendous help to Criswell. He provided a valuable link between the old and the new. The situation is described by historian Leon McBeth:

> Over the years, the First Baptist Church had gradually become a rather staid, downtown church, ministering primarily to mature adults. Most of the deacons were past sixty years of age. The church staff, faithful as they

> were, was by no means numerous enough to carry a full-family centered church program. Much of the staff work rested in the hands of Bob Coleman and T. A. Johnson, both outstanding and eminently loyal men but both of advanced age.[2]

Criswell did not want to neglect any of the older members of the church. He simply wanted to rebuild the image and ministry of the historic church. Criswell's desire was to create a family-centered church program that would appeal to young families and their children:

> There was a very noticeable emphasis upon the youth of the First Baptist Church when Dr. Criswell began his pastorate. Each year a "youth-week" was conducted in the month of June. During the week a group of young people, selected by the church, had complete charge of the church program. For instance, one young man would be the pastor, taking Dr. Criswell's place, another was the choir director, another was the Educational Director, etc. This unusual program has helped the young people to realize the enormous task of planning and carrying out the work of a great church and to visualize the fields of service open to them. It also helped the older members of the church to realize that the church had talented young people who were willing to consecrate themselves to tasks of primary importance. Above all, it enabled the church to look to a great future under the leadership of their young people. Two notable evangelists of our day, Howard Butt and Buckner Fanning, were at one time "Youth Pastors" at the First Baptist Church. An outstanding recording artist for Word Records, Frank Boggs, grew up in the church and had many opportunities to act as choir director during "Youth Week."[3]

Each time the leadership of the church met, the elderly deacons would listen to their young pastor as he unfolded his dreams for the future. After he finished they would begin to explain to him why his goals and dreams would not work. "Pastor, all that sounds wonderful, it might work at other places, but not here. You see, this is an old downtown church—we reach mainly adults. The young people and young families go to the suburban churches."[4]

The deacons had not yet learned that Criswell was not easily dissuaded. He would not give up. He felt he was trying to accomplish the work of God, not simply his own ideals. This is the reason the drive and determination of Criswell is so strong. From the pulpit, at deacons' meetings, and in private visits with individual members, he presented the dreams of a complete, well-rounded, family-centered church program in downtown Dallas. Criswell knew that if the great downtown church was destined to survive it had to become a family church. But he continued to meet opposition. After some days had passed, Criswell's program was presented to the deacons for a formal vote. The future of Criswell's entire ministry rode on that one vote.

Judge Frank Ryburn was chairman of the Board of Deacons. He had been one of the seven members of the pulpit committee who recommended Criswell be called as the new pastor. He supported Criswell and his plans for the future of the church. McBeth recounts the meeting:

> After warm discussion, Chairman Frank Ryburn said, "As for me, I am going with the pastor." He then asked all the others who would back Criswell's program to stand, and all but two men stood immediately to their feet. It may have seemed routine at the time, but this was one of the most significant victories Criswell ever won. From that moment he had his opportunity to see what he could build in Dallas.[5]

No sooner had Criswell been given the opportunity to move ahead when potential problems arose:

> A crisis came when a leading member rather casually proposed an absolute ceiling of $200,000.00 on church indebtedness. What this meant was that Criswell would be unable to build the kind of church-wide ministry he envisioned.
>
> Deacon Charlie Roberts, vice-president of Sears Roebuck, who had just led the vast expansion of that firm and thus understood expansion, stood by the pastor. He went to the member who proposed the limit and said very frankly, "Either get in with us or get out." It was spoken kindly, but in straight frankness. The result was that the church did not adopt the restrictive ceiling.[6]

Dr. Truett had not insisted on any particular type of church organization. Everything was relatively small, including the staff. McBeth notes that administration of the Sunday school would have frustrated Truett. Bob Coleman was in charge of this area. Coleman was the business symbol; Truett was the spiritual symbol.[7]

Truett had built the church around his pulpit ministry. People came literally from the ends of the earth to hear him speak. He stood tall and erect in the pulpit, never moving, simply preaching on different topics found in the Bible. The church looked upon its own ministry as being the preaching of Dr. Truett. No special attention was given to church growth or expansion.

If Truett had an educational structure perhaps it can best be visualized in Table 1. A particular person was in charge of an area of church life such as Sunday school or Training Union. The person in charge of that particular area headed up that aspect of ministry throughout the entire church, from the youngest to the oldest member. For example, the Sunday school leader led the Sunday school program for the entire church. The Sunday school leader was responsible for the program and the curriculum for every age throughout the church. Regardless of age or category (nursery, beginners, primaries, juniors, youth, or adults) everyone was under the supervision and direction of the Sunday school leader. This same situation existed for every area of church life. One person was responsible for the Sunday school program, another for the Training Union program, and so on, throughout.

Table 1

The Educational Programming Structure of George W. Truett

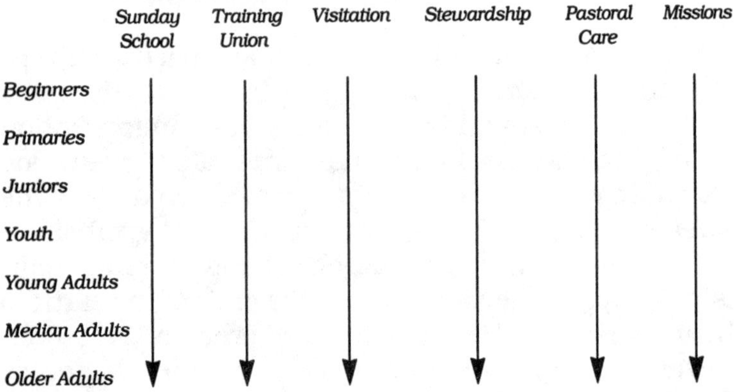

Criswell began to turn things around. As seen in Table 2, he reorganized the church. There would be no Sunday school leader or Training Union leader as such. The church would be divided into graded divisions instead, and leaders would be responsible for leading and directing all the activities within their particular divisions throughout the church. Whoever led an age group would lead it completely. The Divisional Director for a graded age group would be responsible for the Sunday school program (for example, recruiting and training teachers, establishing the curriculum, and visiting the prospects). The Divisional Directors would also be responsible for the Training Union program, the Mission program, raising of financial pledges, pastoral care, and all aspects of church programs throughout their entire division. Criswell thought that in this manner every aspect of church life would be in the hands of responsible individuals who could carefully work with the large numbers of people who were coming into the church.

Table 2

The Educational Programming Structure of W. A. Criswell

	Sunday School	*Training Union*	*Visitation*	*Stewardship*	*Pastoral Care*	*Missions*
Beginners	→	→	→	→	→	→
Primaries	→	→	→	→	→	→
Juniors	→	→	→	→	→	→
Youth	→	→	→	→	→	→
Young Adults	→	→	→	→	→	→
Median Adults	→	→	→	→	→	→
Older Adults	→	→	→	→	→	→

Many years ago when I began the expansion of the church, the staff organization always followed a perpendicular plan. There was a leader for the Sunday School, and a leader for the other groups in the church. I turned the organizational chart over and made it horizontal, with a leader for the age group responsible for his section Sunday morning, Sunday evening in Training Union, and throughout all the activities of the work. This makes for an excellent program, full-rounded, in every age. Instead of the ministry of the church to a child, a youth, or an adult being chopped up by different leaders

> who are furthering their own programs, we have one leader over it all for the age who plans the work throughout the days of the week.[8]

The church has evolved in its structure over the years and continues to do so. Presently the church has eight "sections" of ministry all under the direction of the pastor and the Executive Director of Ministries. The Cabinet, Directors, support ministries, secretaries, and hourly workers all work together for the goals and purposes of the entire First Baptist Church. The current educational structure can be seen in Table 3. The Criswell College and First Baptist Academy are not shown on the chart because both institutions have governing boards that are elected according to their own bylaws. However, one would be naive indeed to believe that Criswell was not the primary supporter and driving force behind both schools.

As seen in Table 3, the pastor of the church is the autocratic leader of the organization. From him emanates a participative (democratic and consultative) leadership style. It is *participative* in the sense that there is an open invitation to share in the ministry of the church. It is *democratic* in the sense that groups work together within the church on specific projects or assignments, each sharing their best ideas. It is *consultative* in that after the groups have discussed issues at hand, the pastor is then consulted in order for him to decide what final action is to be taken. In this scenario only major items of interest are involved. And again, everything is subject to final approval by the Fellowship of Deacons, who usually go along with the pastor's wishes.

Changes began to slowly occur. In 1945, L. H. Tapscott, former Educational Director, overseeing the Training Union program, resigned to become secretary of the Texas Baptist Brotherhood work. In addition, Mrs. J. H.

Table 3

Concentric Zones of Ministries at the First Baptist Church, Dallas

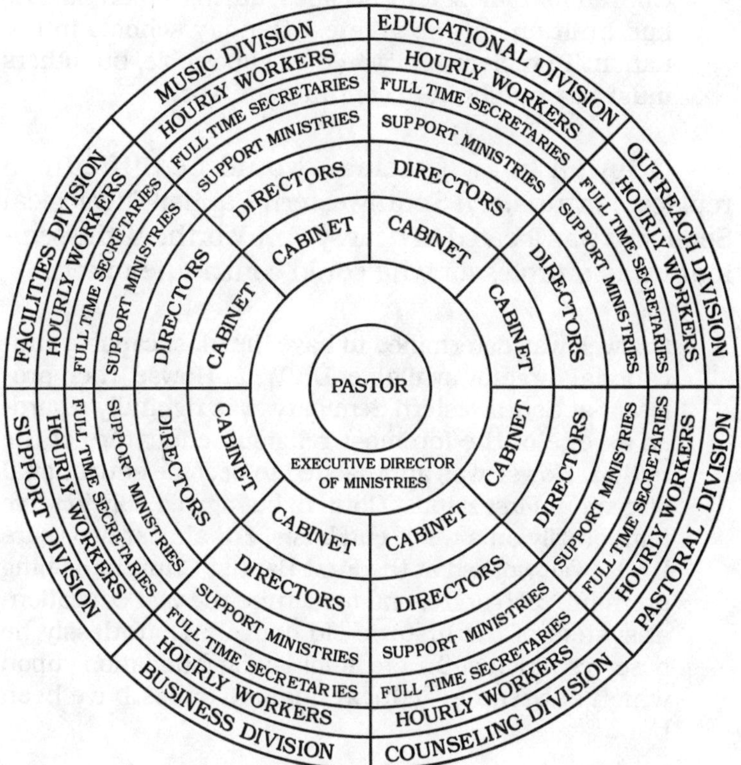

Cassidy, who had been the choir director and church organist for more than twenty-five years, retired.

In the early morning of February 13, 1946, Bob Coleman died, the victim of pneumonia. He was seventy-six years old. Dr. Criswell and E. D. Head of Fort Worth conducted the funeral. It was a difficult assignment for Criswell because he loved Coleman dearly. But again, Truett's words echoed: "God buries the workman, but the work goes on." The final stages of the Truett era and the beginning of the Criswell era were complete:

> With Coleman's death the Truett era was at an end. he had been the educational leader of the First Baptist Church for almost four decades, during which time he had built one of the greatest Sunday schools in the nation. To replace him would be impossible, but others must be brought in to continue the work.[9]

Criswell knew Coleman would be difficult to replace. Fortunately, Southwestern Baptist Theological Seminary was located in nearby Fort Worth. At the seminary was a professor who could contribute much:

> Criswell was determined to have the most capable educational director available. Dr. W. L. Howse, then professor at Southwestern Seminary, was rightfully regarded as one of the foremost religious educators of the nation. Howse was approached to become educational director at First Baptist Church, but agreed only to serve temporarily on a week-end basis. For almost two years Dr. Howse worked at the First Baptist Church, helping overhaul, reorganize, and modernize the vast educational system of the historic old church. Doubtlessly he deserves much of the credit for laying foundations upon which subsequent educational advances have been built.[10]

By 1946 Criswell had been pastor of the church for almost two years. He had earned the complete confidence of his people. The programs that he laid out to the deacons had been accepted. He now began seeking adequate staff to run it on a daily basis. The facilities that would be needed for the church to become family-centered would be built in time.

The interim days were complete. Criswell was at the helm of his ship. The First Baptist Church faced an open door to the future. Criswell assured his people that the best days for the old downtown church and its congregation were still ahead. The pastor was no longer Dr. Truett's "successor." He was W. A. Criswell, powerful preacher and beloved pastor, who enjoyed the unquestioning confidence and support of his people.

As with most great individuals, there comes a point when the person surpasses the position he holds or the institution he represents. When Criswell came to be pastor of First Baptist Church, Dallas, he was virtually unknown. He had held no special position of prominence. Criswell himself felt that he was not in the same league with George W. Truett.

It is important to note Criswell's humility in honoring Truett. Criswell understood how people despise a proud, arrogant leader. However, people will do almost anything in their power to support and follow a man who is a "shepherd," one who leads with a sense of direction but at the same time shows compassion toward people. From the outset of securing support, causing the congregation to want to follow him. An example is his first New Year's message in 1945:

> In the presence of so much to be done and so great a responsibility, your pastor feels like a child. We yield all guidance, all direction, all power, all leadership to our heavenly Father! Oh, God, do thou take us by the hand and lead us along. Keep us from stumbling and from error. Fill our hearts with faith amazing . . . and if thou shalt accept us, we shall go on forever unafraid.[11]

Notice Criswell's use of "we," "our," and "us." He placed himself beside his people, rather than above them, becoming a fellow pilgrim along life's way. This, in turn, caused the people to honor their young, humble pastor and to give him the freedom he would need to lead the church.

In time he learned to function in his new role as the pastor of one of the most prominent churches in the Southern Baptist Convention. Truett's name had become synonymous with First Baptist, Dallas. Now Criswell would face that same challenge. Not only did he rise to the occasion, but in time the roles seemed to switch. No longer was there simply a well-known church with a new pastor, but the pastor became a well-known figure himself. The church began to take on the identity of the pastor. Criswell's involvement in church activities grew to the point where he was associated with numerous aspects of Baptist life. W. A. Criswell began to *be the institution.*

NOTES

1. T. Charlton and R. Spain, *Oral Memoirs of W. A. Criswell* (Waco, Tex.: Baylor Univ. 1973), p. 167.
2. Leon McBeth, *The First Baptist Church of Dallas* (Grand Rapids: Zondervan, 1968), p. 233.
3. R. DuCasse, *A History of the First Baptist Church, Dallas, Texas* (Master's Thesis, Dallas Theological Seminary, 1964), p. 162.
4. McBeth, *The First Baptist Church of Dallas*, pp. 233-34.
5. Ibid., p. 234.
6. Ibid.
7. Ibid., p. 237.
8. W. A. Criswell, *Criswell's Guidebook for Pastors* (Nashville: Broadman, 1980), p. 88.
9. McBeth, *The First Baptist Church of Dallas*, p. 238.
10. Ibid.
11. W. A. Criswell, *The Reminder* (a publication of First Baptist Church), 1 January 1945, p. 4.

5
Educational Contributions

When W. A. Criswell began to rebuild the First Baptist Church he knew it would include more than a one-day-per-week program. He wanted a total church program that would keep Christian education and evangelism at the center of the life of the church. Although the purpose of this book is not to provide a chronological study of the First Baptist Church under Criswell's leadership, the first few years of Criswell's tenure reveal the philosophy of ministry he introduced to the church.

Building Programs

Criswell knew his plan would require additional buildings. By 1946 Criswell began to emphasize this:

> As the carpenter must have his tools to build, so must a church have its tools and equipment if it is to build anything significant. We must have buildings to house our people. We must have more space for our children. We must provide more adequately for our young people. We must obtain more land adjacent to our downtown church for expansion.[1]

At every opportunity Criswell stressed the need for expansion. "With great conviction and contagious enthusiasm, Pastor Criswell proclaimed this mandate for the future. The people listened and they believed. Their response made possible one of the greatest eras of advance in the history of the great church."[2]

When Criswell began his building program emphasis the church owned two buildings: the sanctuary and the building immediately behind it, known at that time as simply the educational building. The educational building had originally been built in 1924 but was never completed on the inside. The building was in a state of repair and renovation during the 1940s. Each floor was gradually being remodeled.

When the building was completed, the deacons voted, at the suggestion of Dr. Criswell, to change the name from the educational building to the Truett Building in honor of their former pastor. At the same time the large downstairs fellowship hall was named Coleman Hall in honor of Robert Coleman. These existing facilities, however still did not suffice for the church program Criswell had in mind.

In May of 1947 the church voted to build an activities building on the corner of Ervay and San Jacinto. This would be the first new church building in more than twenty years. Although a consensus existed to build a new structure, many hindrances occurred. Several changes were made as they proceeded. When the foundation was being dug an underground river was discovered. Building costs had soared over the past quarter century. When ground was finally broken in 1951, the worst delay of all occurred: a shortage of steel due to the Korean War. Restrictions on steel brought construction to a grinding halt. The church members looked at a gigantic hole in the ground for months.

The drive and determination of W. A. Criswell has overcome many obstacles. From childhood he has known adversity. Criswell has become famous not out of "luck" or the turning of fate but out of dedication and perseverance. Proverbs 24:10 states, "If thou faint in the day of adversity, thy strength is small." Criswell refuses to faint and demonstrates great strength.

Finally in 1952, eighteen carloads of steel girders were loaded and marked for Dallas. But due to a railroad strike, further delays were encountered. At last the steel rolled into Dallas. Construction progressed swiftly. By the end of 1953, the building was ready for occupancy. Members were invited to furnish offices, parlors, or classrooms. Plaques in their names lined the walls as memorials. Most of the money was raised in this manner. A few large donations were received, including a $40,000 gift by the four daughters of Colonel C. C. Slaughter, for whom one of the chapels was named.

The facility was immediately put into full use. Sunday school space was utilized to the fullest capacity, as was office space. A tunnel hallway was built under San Jacinto Street to connect the new building with the auditorium basement. In 1959, the church deacons recommended that the beautiful building be known as the Criswell Building. The church body approved, and the *Activities Building* became the *Criswell Building.*

Before the Criswell Building was completed, W. A. Criswell began his next campaign. Criswell saw the need for adequate parking facilities, especially on weekdays. Even in the early 1950s, however, land was very expensive in downtown Dallas, and the church did not want to go any farther into debt.

Then the Central Christian Church, located on the corner of St. Paul and San Jacinto, went up for sale. This facility was right across the street from the First Baptist Church. Criswell wanted that property, and he was convinced that God wanted the church to have that location. He knew if a business purchased it and built on it, the location would be lost forever. The asking price of the property was $260,000. Criswell often recounts the situation:

I was standing on Patterson Street looking at a sign on the Central Christian Church which read "For Sale." They had decided to move out into the suburbs. They had a quarter of a block of property on which their church was built. At that time we were in the building program of what you now call the Criswell Building. I went to our Fellowship of Deacons and said, "Some corporation will buy that property and build a fifty-story building on it and we will never possess it. Now is the time to buy it. Let's buy it." And the deacons unanimously replied to me, "We are already with more financial obligations than we [can handle]. . . . We cannot entertain the idea of buying this Central Christian Church."

I was standing there with Billy Souther, our Educational Director at that time, and I said to Mr. Souther, "I want you to look at that. That is the saddest sight in all this world. That property is for sale, and if we do not buy it we will never possess it. . . . I have asked the Deacons to buy it and the Deacons unanimously refused." Mr. Souther looked at me and said, "Why don't you ask God for it?"

"Well," I said to him, "I never had thought of that. I thought you would have to ask the deacons for it!"

"Well," he said,"why don't you try asking God for it?" I thought I would try.

After I had been praying about that for a few weeks, I received a telephone call from Mrs. Minnie Slaughter Veal. She said to me, "I hear you are down on your face praying. What are you praying for?"

I said, "Mrs. Veal, I am praying that God will give our church that Central Christian Church property that is up for sale."

She said, "Well, how much is it?"

I said, "I don't know, but I will find out real soon!" I found out and called her back.

She said, "You buy it and I will give you the money for it."

So, in about a week or two she called me again and said, "By the way, I forgot to ask you. . . . What do you want that property for?"

I said, "I want to build a parking building on it. And on top of the parking building I want to build a facility where our people can come be together: a gymnasium, a skating rink, bowling lanes, and hamburger joint."

She said to me, "Well, how much will that cost?"

I said, "I don't know but I will tell you real soon!" I called her back and said, "The architect said that it will cost a million five hundred thousand dollars."

She said, "You build that building and I will give you the money."

I built that building and the church did not even know what was going on.[3]

In *The First Baptist Church of Dallas*, Leon McBeth notes:

> This good woman put out over a quarter million dollars without even knowing what the pastor had in mind! That is one of the most remarkable demonstrations of confidence in Criswell in his tenure at First Baptist Church. When Mrs. Veal knew of the details of the property's use, she was even more enthusiastic. In fact, she gave a total of $1,755,500.00 for this building which did not cost the church a penny. If the Criswell Building was the hardest the church ever obtained, the Veal Building was probably the easiest. Not for about a year did the church even know who the donor of this building was, for she wished to remain anonymous.[4]

Now Criswell had the facilities he desired. In addition to the sanctuary and the Truett Building, which had recently been remodeled and completed, he now had the Criswell Building and a parking building with facilities for the youth and recreation program he wanted. A dedication for the new buildings was held early in 1954. An entire Sunday was devoted to the dedication ceremonies.

Facilities were merely tools to Criswell, implementing the multifaceted programs of the church. Criswell saw programs simply as people in action: people learning, praying, giving, going, playing, and worshiping. Programs, through the years, give life and excitement to the church and help the people grow.

It is evident that Criswell equates activity and involvement with growth and productivity. In order to get results there must be activity. The more activity, the greater the results. If a little is good, a lot more is better. More can't be done with less, but more *can* be done with more. Churches don't have a money problem, they have a people problem. Get more people and the money will follow. Missionary William Carey said, "Attempt great things for God, expect great things from God."[5] These thoughts and expressions characterize Criswell's philosophy in building a great church.

Preaching and Growing

As early as 1946 Criswell had begun a great preaching campaign. He believed in his heart that people were hungry to hear the Word of God taught, and when it was, the church would grow. Truett had been a topical preacher. He had never preached through a book of the Bible verse by verse. Most preachers in Truett's era were topical preachers.

In Muskogee, as you will recall, Criswell had changed his preaching. From the notes given to him from Dr. Hall's library, Criswell began to develop his messages in a different manner. The response had been encouraging. In March of 1946, the young pastor began preaching a series entitled "The Plan of Salvation Through the Ages." His announced goal was to preach through the entire Bible verse by by verse, which ultimately took him eighteen years.

> We are asking the Holy Spirit to guide us into all truth, to show forth in each book the unveiling of Christ and

> the redemptive purposes of God. We shall feast upon the Word. Could it be, oh, could it be that God might take these sermons and use them to kindle a fire that shall burn in our hearts until the whole world shall be blessed by the Spirit's presence and power among us?[6]

In looking back over those early days Criswell is amused. Not only did the church membership think he had lost his mind, they thought it would be the undoing of his seemingly successful new ministry.

> You never heard such lugubrious proliferation in your life. Even the finest deacon that I had said, "You will clear the church. Nobody is coming here to listen to a sermon on Haggai, Zechariah or Malachi. I don't even know where they are found in the Bible!"
>
> They were correct in one instance. The people had never heard sermons from Haggai, Zechariah, or Malachi. And they were right about having another problem with crowds. But the problem was the people could not get into the sanctuary. There was not enough room! That is why after I had been here about three years we began having two services on Sunday morning, one at 8:15 and one at 10:50 to accommodate the people that wanted to come to listen to an exposition of the Word of God.[7]

Criswell set out on his preaching journey believing with all his heart that there would be a vigorous response to the verse-by-verse teaching of the Word of God.

> The first three and a half years Criswell preached through the Old Testament. On September 12, 1949, he began in the New Testament and spent almost a year on the first nine chapters of Matthew. In February of 1953, he finished the four Gospels. For over seven years, he preached through the Acts and Epistles, and on December 4, 1960, he came to Revelation. For almost three

> years he preached through the twenty-one chapters of this mysterious concluding book of the Bible. At the completion of the entire series, the young and median adult department presented the Pastor a beautiful Bible on his nineteenth anniversary in appreciation for his almost eighteen years series.[8]

The crowds began to come, and the church began to grow. Criswell used his ingenuity to gather people. To him it seemed that people enjoyed being part of a big cause. Whether building programs or preaching series, people seemed to like being part of a team effort that had a definite goal.

As the adults came to hear Criswell preach they brought their children with them. The Sunday school began to experience phenomenal growth. It became the lead organization that set the pace for the entire church program. Criswell remembered his earlier pastoring days at Marlow Baptist Church when he was only eighteen years old. The parents came to the church because their children wanted to come. Criswell would forever place a strong emphasis on the youth, from the nursery through the teenage years. He had seen it succeed repeatedly in building the church. The youth did not make up 100 percent of the church family, but they did make up 100 percent of the church future.

The old staff Criswell inherited could not handle the crowds and new growth the church was experiencing. He began looking for a permanent director of education to replace W. L. Howse, who taught in the School of Religious Education at the Southwestern Baptist Theological Seminary.

> The quality of Howse's work is seen in the fact that the pastor and church repeatedly invited him to assume a regular staff position. After six months Howse resigned to devote more time to his seminary work. However, those were valuable months. In a way they were tran-

sitional. The Sunday School was totally reorganized, and geared for the advance which came steadily in later years. Perhaps Howse's greatest contribution was in laying foundations for a vast program of teacher training. Without this the growth of later years would have been greatly handicapped.[9]

After Bob Coleman died in 1946, the church was without a Sunday school superintendent and a music director (since Coleman had led the singing in the church services as well). One of the new desires of Criswell was to upgrade and modernize the music ministry. In June 1946 W. H. Souther joined the staff as both minister of music and director of education. Souther came to Dallas from the First Baptist Church of San Antonio. Criswell had high hopes that Souther would take up where Bob Coleman had left off.

> Souther will be our Brother Bob Coleman. He will direct the entire educational, promotional, enlistment, and music program of our great church. What the chief of staff is to an army, Mr. Souther will be to our First Baptist Church. Everything will be committed to his wise leadership and able counsel. . . . If ever a man had a big job, Mr. Souther has it.[10]

Although Souther did a magnificent job with the music, the Sunday school program is where he excelled. Since Criswell wanted to grade the Sunday school program by age division, Souther followed through and in time organized the Sunday school program on a graded-age-group basis. This made the educational program of the church fit nicely with the overall church direction. From nursery through adult, modern educational methods of instruction and interaction were employed.

The church experienced fantastic growth under the leadership and direction of Mr. Souther. People were coming, the pastor was preaching, buildings were going up, and a spirit of anticipation permeated the air. Souther worked at the church for twelve years, then went to teach music at New Orleans Baptist Theological Seminary. Criswell is quick to pour accolades on people. He shares his glory with his co-workers. Accordingly, later, in 1967, when Souther was a visiting guest of the church, Criswell said, "The guiding genius of the Sunday school program as we know it is Billy Souther."

But the real driving force behind the scenes was W. A. Criswell. When Criswell came to be the pastor he had required two things: freedom in the pulpit to preach whatever he felt God led him to say (and to appoint a representative to preach in his place during any absence), and control over the staff. Everything in the pulpit was fine. Now it was time to build a staff.

> One of the greatest victories for Criswell and the church was winning the church leaders to the idea of building a top-notch specialized church staff. For all its greatness, the old First Church had never had an adequate staff. Criswell's program depended upon enlistment of people to lead it. However, the deacons were startled at the number of helpers Criswell wanted. At the June meeting of deacons in 1947 Criswell reported on the status of the staff, once again appealing for more help. After lengthy discussion the deacons voted to give the pastor a free hand to build a staff as he saw the need. Few votes have been more important to the pastor.[11]

Two of the earliest hired employees were Mrs. Gladys Browning as Young People's Director and Miss Natalie LaRoe as Intermediate Director. Criswell was trying to place the work of the graded program into the hands of capable individuals who would handle the entire responsibility for their age group from beginning to end. It appears from the very start that Criswell had an affinity for female leadership in his staff. "Criswell's inclinations to heed female advice, while at the same time neglecting that of his masculine associates, in all likelihood owes its origin to his affinities with his mother."[12] At any rate, Criswell's goal of obtaining a professionally trained staff for each age group began to be a reality.

> This program made possible a much more intensive Sunday School program at First Baptist Church, not to mention the correlation of all activities as each age group. By their special programs these age group directors prepared the older children for evangelism. They also by planning a superb overall program for each age inculcated a sense of confidence in parents that First Baptist Church provided their children with the very best. This helped enlist members from all over Dallas County.[13]

Truett's philosophy had been to do most of the work of the church himself. Whereas Truett would do the work of ten men, Criswell hired ten men to do the work, thus freeing himself to build the church.

In 1944 the records indicate that the church grew in membership by a total of 419 people (see Appendix C). By 1952 Criswell had led the congregation to expand their vision: 892 people joined that year. In 1953, with new facilities, several new staff members, and the church growing through expositional preaching, it was time for an all-out effort to expand. Much of the genius of Criswell has been to keep people part of a "big cause." Some type of program must be going on at virtually every moment in which people may feel a part.

In 1952, the pastor, Mr. Souther, the graded age group director, and the deacons began planning for an enlargement campaign for 1953. Criswell noted that the project would be in the forefront of the church life for the entire year: "We are to eat, breathe, talk, sleep, walk, drink, dream, and push the Sunday school."[14]

The campaign began in January 1953 with a three-day leadership conference led by W. L. Howse and J. N.

Barnette, both experts in Sunday school work. But, again, the key to the success of the program would prove to be the drive and determination of W. A. Criswell. When Criswell sets his mind to a task he is like a locomotive driving swiftly and powerfully down the tracks. He hates failure more than most men. The late Vince Lombardo once said, "Winning is not everything. It is the only thing."[15] This accurately sums up Criswell's position.

Although the youth program was strong and in place, the adult Sunday school program was in need of reorganization:

> The Sunday School was reorganized as well as enlarged. For decades First Baptist Church adults had been grouped into large, semi-independent Bible classes without regard to age. These classes elected their own teachers, received and disbursed their own funds, and often met downtown at some site removed from the church. Some of them, like the Cranfill class, conducted their own radio broadcast. Others, like the Baraca class, had their own major benevolent project, which often raised more than $10,000.00 each Christmas for the Buckner Children's Home.[16]

Criswell knew the graded program was working well with the youth. The directors he had implemented were responsible for every aspect of church life for those in their division. Why wouldn't this work for the adult program as well?

> The newer method, the one favored by Criswell and Souther, called for adult classes to be grouped into departments, based on age. This was thought to make for better teaching, and for better organization since it brought the Sunday School into closer relation to the total church program and gave the church the prerogative of electing teachers. This was also the method

> being recommended strongly by Baptist Sunday School leaders in Nashville. In fact, these Nashville leaders gave great encouragement and help to grading the Dallas school, for such a prominent achievement would help to lead other churches to do the same.[17]

In time the adult program became graded in its emphasis. (For a complete listing of the graded program, see Appendix D.)

There were some classes, however, that did not want to change, and they still exist. Criswell called this area of the Sunday school program, which was not graded by age, the "Bible Division." The emphasis in this area is on the teacher rather than the age of the adult participant. Some of the outstanding teachers and speakers in the church who lead these classes at the present time include Mrs. W. A. Criswell, nationally known motivational speaker Zig Ziglar, Paige Patterson (president of the Criswell College), and psychologist Dr. Charles Lowery. (For a complete listing of the Bible Division, see Appendix E.)

By the end of 1953, church enrollment surpassed the 6,000 mark for the first time in the church's history. Total gifts had passed the $1 million mark and would never fall below that amount again (see Appendix C). Total additions to church membership for the year approached the 1,000 mark.

Although Criswell was younger than most of his deacons, he strove for an excellent Board of Deacons who would work closely with him in implementing the financial and functional work of the church. At times he did not get all the cooperation he desired. When that occurred he looked for alternative ideas.

> The youthful pastor, representative of a new generation, felt the deacon body could use a bit of organizational updating along with the Sunday School and the church

> generally. However, the first plans for these changes did not appeal to the deacons. For example, when a proposal was made to begin a deacon rotation system early in 1945, the move was tabled despite its backing by the pastor. The next year Criswell suggested dividing the deacons into two groups, one primarily for administrative work and the other primarily as an activities board. After lengthy discussion, no action was taken.[18]

When Criswell faced obstacles he did not give up. He simply looked for another method by which he might implement his ideas. Criswell enjoys working with people who are visionary. (On more than one occasion Criswell has said, "If the deacons had gone along with me our church would now own the entire northwest quadrant of Dallas county.")

In December 1946, Criswell recommended the formation of a "Junior Board" of deacons. These young men in their twenties and thirties would be elected the same way as the older deacons. However, they would not be ordained as deacons but simply function as an activities board to assist the pastor. The action passed overwhelmingly. Thus, in January 1947 one of the most significant groups in the history of the church came into existence.

This group collectively exhibits the servant's heart of the pastor. Their job is to open doors, drive buses, assist the handicapped, help with the Sunday evening offering, lend a helping hand, and love and serve the people. "The Junior Board also brought some of the finest young men into more active service of the church. Understandably, this group came to be a prime recruiting ground for new deacons at First Baptist Church."[19]

One of Criswell's methods for church growth could be clearly seen in the idea of making people feel welcome when they came to church. First Baptist Church was not to be thought of as the "big downtown church," but as the "big friendly church."

Roundup

In 1945, Criswell devised a plan for "rounding up" all the church members at summer's end, getting them ready to enter the fall program with much enthusiasm. Naturally, this week became known as "Roundup." The families came down to the church each evening for a ranch-style dinner, activities, and a program with a Western theme. Criswell loves large crowds in close quarters, where people can greet and fellowship with one another. His first invitation to Roundup was, "Come in ranch clothes or come as you are—it's the fun sensation of the century—games, music, eats, fun!"[20]

Of course, the church responded. The program has expanded and varied over the years from extravaganzas under a big tent on the downtown church property, to out-of-the-city festivities at a dude ranch and a "First Baptist Only" night at Six Flags over Texas. Criswell's formula for success can again be seen: activity plus involvement equals growth and productivity. Many churches throughout the Southern Baptist Convention now have "Roundup" to get off to a good start for the fall season.

Family Camp

In July of 1949 Criswell introduced the church to its first "All-Church Encampment Week." Criswell wanted the families of the church to have a time to build closer relationships with each other and with Jesus Christ through recreation, Bible study, preaching, and a time spent alone with God. In 1948, the church erected a lodge on land owned by the Dallas Baptist Association known as the Mount Lebanon Assembly twenty-one miles south of downtown Dallas on Highway 167. In April of 1949 the new lodge was dedicated. Over the years the camp grounds have evolved primarily into youth facilities for summer camps. However, many adult groups use Mount Lebanon on the weekends.

Criswell is interested in much more than simply having a lot of activity. He is not interested in a large group of people just for the sake of gathering a crowd. The motive underlying Criswell's methods is an evangelistic spirit. Dr. Criswell has always kept the goal of winning people to Christ at the very center of his ministry. This goal has always been at the center of the total church program under Criswell's supervision.

Revival Days

Criswell began spring revival campaigns as soon as he arrived as the new pastor. As early as 1949 tremendous effects were being felt by the church as a result of these revival meetings:

> By any measurement this 1949 revival must be counted a success. The closing Sunday service lasted from 9:30 to 1:00 o'clock. Joining the church were 306 people, 130 of them first time converts. Someone joined the church at every service during the month except the third Tuesday night. Eight young persons dedicated their lives to some form of Christian ministry. This was a presage of the future when the First Baptist Church would be a major recruiting ground among Baptists for ministerial students.[21]

In 1950 Criswell was preaching in North Carolina. He went to the home of a young, up-and-coming evangelist by the name of Billy Graham. After a long talk and a meal together, Criswell was convinced God's hand was upon the young man. On January 7, 1951, Billy Graham came to the First Baptist Church in Dallas to preach. By 1953 Graham had been thrust into national prominence by the Los Angeles Crusade. When Graham returned to Dallas for a revival in 1953 the church could not contain the crowds. The meeting had to be moved to the nearby Cotton Bowl. At the end of the week Criswell and the church in Dallas experienced a wonderful event. Graham, who was attending the Sunday morning service, came forward during the invitation time and placed his membership in the First Baptist Church. Graham wanted to be identified with the tremendous evangelistic fervor of the church. He has remained a member there ever since.

STEWARDSHIP

In the fall of every year, right after Roundup when most of the people are back in church on a regular basis, the annual stewardship campaign begins. No program at First Baptist Church receives more detailed planning or more careful promotion than the stewardship campaign.

Criswell has always been active in the stewardship program, preaching sermons from biblical passages on stewardship and encouraging every person from the oldest to the youngest to participate. However, he refuses to be responsible for the entire program. Most of the details fall into the hands of the finance committee and the divisional directors. A stewardship theme is adopted and a chairman is elected by the congregation at the Finance Committee's recommendation. Then the process of pledging gifts to the church for the following year begins.

Every person in the church falls into a Sunday school category, even if only in the group known as "Church members not enrolled in Sunday school." Criswell believes that people do what is "inspected" rather than what is "expected." A Divisional Director is over each area of the church. He insists that the directors personally give each member the opportunity to turn in a pledge card. Over the years the program has varied only slightly.

> The third Sunday in November is known as Victory Sunday. Every member present is asked to turn in his pledge card indicating what he will give to all church causes during the next year. Members unable to be present are asked to mail their pledge cards, and hundreds do. After the morning service, the pastor and men of the church have lunch in Coleman Hall, and then divide into visitation teams to call on members who have not yet turned in pledge cards.[22]

Many preachers have developed a reputation for preaching about money too often. It was even the practice of Truett to raise money throughout the year by special appeal for certain projects (foreign missions, home missions, Buckner Children's Home, etc.). Except for an emergency or some special project, Criswell rarely "browbeats" people regarding money. His emphasis is on the yearly stewardship campaign.

> It will surprise you how very seldom I refer to any of the financial programs of the church. I do it so infrequently that one year the Finance Committee came to me, the Stewardship Committee came to me and asked me to say something about it in the pulpit. I rarely refer to it, rarely, but the heart of the church is in sympathy with a tithing appeal and my own heart of course is.[23]

NOTES

1. Leon McBeth, *The First Baptist Church of Dallas* (Grand Rapids: Zondervan, 1968), p. 234.
2. Ibid., p. 243.
3. W. A. Criswell, "Walking by Faith Alone," sermon preached at First Baptist Church, 3 December 1986.
4. McBeth, *The First Baptist Church of Dallas*, p. 269.
5. M. Drewery, *William Carey: A Biography* (Grand Rapids: Zondervan, 1981), p. 88.
6. W. A. Criswell, *The Reminder* (publication of First Baptist Church) 3 March 1946, p. 1.
7. W. A. Criswell, "Founder's Day Message," sermon preached at

First Baptist Church, 29 September 1987.

8. McBeth, *The First Baptist Church of Dallas*, p. 338.
9. Ibid., p. 252.
10. Ibid.
11. Ibid., pp. 261-62.
12. Paige Patterson, "The Imponderables of God," *Criswell Theological Review 1*, no. 2: 239.
13. McBeth, *The First Baptist Church of Dallas*, p. 253.
14. Ibid., p. 254.
15. J. Kramer, *Lombardi: Winning Is the Only Thing* (New York: Pocket Books, 1971), p. i.
16. McBeth, *The First Baptist Church of Dallas*, p. 254.
17. Ibid., p. 255.
18. Ibid., p. 260.
19. Ibid., p. 261.
20. W. A. Criswell, *The Reminder*, 3 March 1946, p. 3.
21. McBeth, *The First Baptist Church of Dallas*, p. 254.
22. Ibid., p. 248.

6
Further Expansion

As time passed it became apparent that even though First Baptist Church was located in an expensive area of town, it had to expand. The church was fast becoming the reality of Criswell's dream, namely a family-centered ministry. Enrollment was expanding yearly (see Appendix C), so the church began looking for ways to increase their facilities.

The Burt Building

Next door to the sanctuary was an office building owned by R. E. Burt. The building was an eleven-story structure with 90,000 square feet of space. For some time Criswell had wanted the church to purchase the building, but the price kept it out of reach. Finally Mr. Burt had a change of heart:

> The owner, R. E. Burt, agreed to sell for $1,000,000.00, far below the appraised market value. His willingness to sell to the First Baptist Church, especially at that price, ranks as one of the most significant property transactions in the history of this great church. This also proved the last major building of the church's first century.[1]

At last the church had some room to expand in a big way. But Criswell never sees a big opportunity as an end in itself. He sees big opportunities as means to bigger opportunities:

> Since the building was not designed for church use, all floors required extensive remodeling. Pastor Criswell said, "It will take time to work out the use of the Burt Building and to fit it into the overall educational program." His illustration was that a boy does not grow just in his thumb and his toe, but all over. A church grows the same way. More space for children would not help unless at the same time more room could be made for their parents. Or as Pastor Criswell put it, "We cannot just grow in the Young Married departments without also growing in the nursery area. Expansion in one department calls for expansion in all departments."[2]

Some people in leadership positions thought the purchase of the Burt Building was a good idea from an investment point of view. The building could be used as a lucrative piece of rental property and in a few years would pay for itself. Criswell's thoughts about that idea were quite pointed: "Our Church is not in the office renting business. We bought the Burt Building to make room for an expanding Sunday School."[3]

Criswell knew the church could not expand further or go deeper into debt. But he wanted to impart his philosophical views to the people. This is a key concept to grasp. He was not about to quit expanding. The seeds he planted in the minds of the people would grow in time. When he thought the time was right for the next expansion, perhaps they would be ready to go along with their visionary pastor.

With the opening of the Burt Building came the opportunity for change, new structures, and expansion:

> The adult division was totally reorganized. For all its emphasis upon young people and children, the First Baptist Church did not forget its adults. They were divided into four divisions in 1960: Young Adults, Median Adults, Senior Adults, and the Independent Class division. Three of these had their own staff director.[4]

The new building also afforded new space for the Juniors and Youth. The Junior Division (made up of fourth, fifth, and sixth graders), and the Youth Division (made up of grades seven through twelve) began to expand rapidly. As time passed, the Sunday school program was subdivided into school grade departments. This follows a trend favored by many churches of structuring Sunday schools to fit the public school grading system.

Nursery Day School and Pre-Easter Services

In 1963 the Nursery Day School opened, providing weekday care for children of working mothers. In 1964 the five-year-old kindergarten program began. Criswell did not see these programs as an end in themselves. He saw them as opportunities to reach out and make new acquaintances with people in the downtown metroplex. He knew many people's first experiences with a church came about through various means. Perhaps one of these extracurricular activities would afford an opportunity to bring new families into the life of the church.

Each year, the week prior to Easter at the noon lunch hour, Criswell brings a series of sermons simply known as the "Pre-Easter Services." For years the meeting took place in downtown Dallas at the Palace Theater (see Appendix F, nos. 18, 30, 33, 36). In later years the meeting moved its location to the church sanctuary. Business people from all over the downtown community attend the meeting. Lunch is served at the church before and after the service for a nominal charge. For most of these people, it is their first exposure to the downtown First Baptist Church. Many of them eventually find their way in to church membership. This is simply another method Criswell uses to reach people for the Lord and the church.

"Spurgeon" Harris Building

As the church began to grow and expand, Criswell knew more facilities would become necessary. In 1969 the eleven-story Internal Revenue Service building across the street from the church was purchased. Actually, the original transaction was a ninety-nine-year lease with a purchase option in the future. This building was a key acquisition; not only was the location important, but this building had several levels for parking. Criswell's keen business mind looks for ways not only to allow the church to grow, but also for methods of income to help it in the process, when appropriate. The parking could be leased out to businesses during the week and used freely by the church members on Sundays. But the deal made Criswell uncomfortable for several years. Although the rent was minimal, he was concerned about the future.

Criswell believes a business or some other type organization may come and go, but the organization of the church will be here forever. Therefore, he wanted the church to purchase the property on which the building was located and eliminate the lease. But this building was expensive. The pastor appealed to the congregation for the funds, explaining the philosophy that the church would "forever" be a downtown church. As previously noted, Criswell is a master in paying tribute to other people. In this manner Criswell gets other people to join him in the cause at hand, thus crowning his efforts with success. Criswell honored the founding pastor of the church, "Spurgeon" Harris, by naming the building after him:

We stand at the beginning of our greatest and noblest year. This church is indelibly identified with a man named W. W. "Spurgeon" Harris. . . . When that boy was 17 years old W. W. Harris was saved and baptized. He seemingly had a gift of language of speech, and he was licensed to preach when he was 17. When he was 21 years of age a Baptist Association took up a collection for him and sent him to the University called Baylor on the Brazos at Independence. When he was 30 years old he preached a Commencement Sermon at Baylor in 1866 entitled, "The Knowledge of Jesus, the Most Excellent of All Scientists." And because of his eloquence they nicknamed him Spurgeon. He was the most successful preacher in Texas. He baptized B. H. Carroll, who founded our Southwestern Seminary in Ft. Worth, Texas. In 1868 in July, this young preacher came to a frontier village in North Texas called Dallas and he held a two week revival meeting in this frontier village. They had one conversion and at the end of the meeting, they organized a Baptist church—the First Baptist Church of Dallas, with ten coming into the fellowship by letter. There were eleven and he was the first pastor. He never resigned upon a day—he just left, and no one knew where he went; he just left. . . . He became an itinerant preacher of the Gospel. . . . He had no family, no means, no voice, no health, and he died of tuberculosis at the age of 44.

He had in his life one of the saddest providences I have ever read about. He was in the Civil War . . . and in those four bloody years he constantly corresponded with a young lady school teacher, whom he was to marry after the war was over. When the war was done he came back to Texas to marry that young woman whom he so loved. When he arrived he found that she had suddenly and impulsively married someone else. It was a crushing blow for his life. He never expressed interest in anyone else—in any other woman—and lived alone until his death at 44 years of age in South Texas. He was buried at Fort San Felipe across the River from Del Rio. There was no marker—no place known—and when I came here to Dallas I told Mr. Tapscott, "I want you to go to South Texas—to

> Del Rio—and I want you to find that place and with God's help and grace we're going to build a marker and a monument to Spurgeon Harris, the first pastor of this church and the organizer of this congregation." After L. H. Tapscott tried for endless times and efforts, he finally came back to me and said, "Pastor, there is no way we can identify the grave of Spurgeon Harris. It cannot be found." So he lies in an unmarked grave, the organizer and pastor of this First Baptist Church in Dallas. I resolved to keep his memory alive here in this place by naming the building across the street the "Spurgeon" Harris Building. And I am so grateful that our congregation acquiesced in that appeal. And always I pray that there will be some remembrance of that lonely, pioneer preacher as long as this church shall last . . . till Jesus comes again.[5]

The congregation answered that appeal through the regular giving program of the church. The building became church property.

President of the Southern Baptist Convention

As the years passed, Criswell's leadership ability, reputation, and influence began to spread. He preached at state evangelistic conferences all over the Southern and Southwestern states. He was nominated several times to be president of the Southern Baptist Convention, but withdrew his name each time. Finally he had a change of heart:

> As time went on I just had that strange conviction that you can't explain, just one of those things that comes from God or out of the blue or sky or whatever. I just had the strange conviction that that was something that I ought to do. So, they nominated me at Houston and I was elected there. And I served as President of the Convention in 1969, and the Convocation was in New Orleans. And then in 1970 and the Convocation was at Denver.[6]

Criswell as a boy (left), with younger brother Currie.

Criswell in later childhood (left), with younger brother Currie.

Criswell's mother and father.

Criswell as a teenager.

Upon graduation from Southern Baptist Theological Seminary, 1934.

Criswell as a young preacher.

W. A. and Betty as a young married couple.

Criswell when he came to Dallas in 1944.

W. A. and Betty in Dallas.

Dedication of the Truett Building picturing (left to right) Marshall Craig, Wallace Bassett, and W. A. Criswell.

Criswell on a mission trip to the Auca indians in Brazil.

Pastor Criswell speaking to his people.

Criswell receiving his honorary doctorate from Liberty University.

W. A. Criswell, lifelong advocate of biblical inerrancy.

The "strange conviction" was probably related to Criswell's awareness that a liberal drift was occurring in the Southern Baptist convention:

> I deplore, as you would know, any leftward drift in the Convention. . . . There's no way it didn't drift to the left. Getting a little more liberal, a little more modern, a little more inclined to accept what men thought rather than what God said. . . . So I knew that when I was nominated that it would be bitterly opposed by the men who wanted to see it drift that way and were encouraging it that way. So I felt that my nomination and election, if it came, would be a decided slowing down of that liberal drift.[7]

Criswell never left the desire to first and foremost be a pastor. All Southern Baptist churches are autonomous in their church polity. Therefore, the position of president does not directly affect each local church. The president's primary responsibility is to make appointments to the various boards and committees. He has no inherent or judicial powers. There are no by-laws, charters, or constitutions that give him power over anything on a daily basis. (There are, however, active powers while the Convention is in session.) He is merely a man of influence because he has been chosen by his peers as a representative of the denomination.

Criswell fulfilled his obligation to the Convention but never got overly involved in the process:

> The presidency of the convention is something of whatever you would choose to do. You can be gone every day, day and night, speaking if you would let them. But I was resolved that there was not going to be anything to take away from the church, my pastorate, in the two years that I was allowed to be President of the Convention.[8]

During the first years of Criswell's presidency his book was released entitled *Why I Preach the Bible Is Lit-*

erally True. There was no confusion as to where Criswell stood. He believes he temporarily turned the movement back to a more conservative position, but he is still concerned about the direction the Convention is headed today. He lays the blame at the feet of the academic community in the seminaries:

> My impression of liberalism and modernism is that it does not come from the people down here who have their dead to bury and their prodigal sons to pray over. Tell a man like that these are parables in the Bible and all that doesn't help him. It's got to be a man that believes something to help people like that in the hour of death and trouble. So my impression is that liberalism never arises from the people. It always arises from a professor who sits in some theological chair and he just sits there. He hardly has any contact with the actual pastoral work of the people. He is in some ivory tower somewhere. He's thinking or philosophizing or something. And so he comes forward with all kinds of ideas and he gets too smart for God. He knows more than God. So he starts spinning out all these things about the Bible, and pretty soon he's accepting this documentary hypothesis and he's teaching Welhausen, Bauer, and all the rest of it. And it isn't long until your young minister has no desire to be a preacher.[9]

Dr. Criswell's term as president came during difficult days for Southern Baptists. Racial riots were occurring in many of the Southern states. He had been accused of being segregationist because of a speech he made to the South Carolina legislature in 1956, advocating segregation.

> I had two things in my mind that led to that expression before the South Carolina legislature. One was, I felt that people ought to have the right of association. That was one thing. If you wanted to form a club of anybody, let's say, fat people, and nobody could belong to that club

> except somebody that weighed over 300 pounds, why that's all right. You could—free country. If you wanted to organize a club of purple people and nobody could join that club except people that were purple in the face, well that's all right. Just whatever you want to do. Whatever you wanted to do in our country, I felt that you ought to have the privilege of doing it. The right of association. You could associate with anybody you wanted to, which meant the obverse of it—you didn't have to associate with anybody you didn't want to. Well, that was one thing.
>
> The other thing that personally just made me seethe on the inside was this: the people that wanted to solve the racial problem in the South were from Harlem and South Chicago and Detroit. And I always said if you're going to have a riot, you're going to have it at Watts in Los Angeles or in South Chicago or in Harlem. And that's all proved true. The big racial explosive situations are in the North, not in the South. There's been very little of it actually in the South compared to how it is up there. Well, I just seethed on the inside when those people up there tell us how to solve the racial problem. Why don't they solve it in Harlem? Why don't they solve it in South Chicago? Why don't they solve it in Watts? Then if they solve it, well, then come down here to the South and tell us. Well, those are the things that led me at times into expressing sentiments about it. But as for being of a turn religiously to segregate people, I never felt that way in my heart. Never. This church, though it was never publicized until I delivered that address on "The Church of the Open Door," the church never, ever thought of doing anything but accepting everybody that God gave to us.[10]

In reality, Criswell was not opposed to blacks or to any other race coming to the downtown church. He simply believed then, as he does now, that most races would rather worship together because of the commonality of their culture.

> I looked upon it pragmatically, and in those days when I was asked about it, I worked over here at West Dallas for years and years and we still have about three missions over there. I'm still working over there. West Dallas is a marginal poor section of town. So I went over there, and I tried to get all those people in one church, in one mission. Well, I just failed completely. So when you divided them up and you had the black people with the black pastor and the Anglo people with an Anglo pastor, and the Mexican people, the Latins with a Latin pastor, why they just flourished over there. They just did great. But when you tried to put them all together, you have a hard time, and eventually failed. That is, I failed in it.[11]

During his term in office, Criswell announced an open door policy for the First Baptist Church by preaching "The Church of the Open Door." The conclusion had been reached earlier by the pastor and the deacons but was never officially announced. Criswell did not want to appear to be "grandstanding" or preaching the sermon simply to get elected president of the Southern Baptist Convention. So, he waited until the 1968 convention had ended to preach the now famous sermon. In the sermon he stated, "The First Baptist Church is now and forever a Philadelphian church of the open door. Anybody can come—and God bless him as he comes."[12]

First Baptist Academy

From the very outset of Criswell's coming to be pastor, he wanted to start a Christian day school, but he immediately ran into opposition from several sources. The leadership of the church did not want to have a Christian school, neither did the leadership of the Baptist General Convention of Texas, nor the leadership of the Southern Baptist Convention in Nashville, Tennessee.[13] Criswell talked to them by the hour but got nowhere:

> They say that we ought not to bring our Christian influence and support out of the public school or that it isn't good for the child to segregate itself, that it grows up narrow and not broad-minded, that the child definitely must face the world that has everybody in it so why pull the child out now and raise him in an unreal world. . . . But I don't believe in that type of thinking. I believe that the child that grows up in a devout Christian home ought to have a devout Christian education. You don't need to worry about what he's going to meet out there in the world. He's going to meet that incidentally. You don't have to feed it into him or put it into him. I don't have to have pneumonia to know all I want to know about it, nor meningitis nor poliomylitis or any other thing. But I'd like to keep my child away from diphtheria, scarlet fever, polio, the whole thing. I'd like to do that same thing for the child.[14]

Criswell did not see his idea as being part of a Baptist parochial system. He simply wanted the church to have its own school. Criswell has a love for education. He was an excellent student in school and continues to strive for knowledge in academic endeavors. But he continued to face opposition.

> I had one of the biggest denominational leaders in the South tell me, "Criswell, I would hate to see you turn aside from being a preacher to a school teacher." He did not say that as being uncomplimentary to a school teacher. He just thought God called me to be a preacher and that I ought not to be a school teacher. And then he elaborated on; he hated to see me turn aside from building the church, winning souls, preparing sermons, praying people into the Kingdom, to running a school with all the problems in a school. Well, I realize all that. There's nothing of that that I hadn't thought through and didn't know before he told me. But I still believe, just as much as I ever did, that what you do in that school is just as important as what I do in that church and what I do in that pulpit.[15]

Another twist of events had occurred that made Criswell want a Christian day school at the church. For many years high school students who enrolled in Old Testament and New Testament survey classes at church received credit toward public school education. This program ended in the late '60s because of pressure brought by the Anti-Defamation League of Dallas.

Finally, in 1972, an interesting turn of events occurred. Nolan Estes, who was with the Federal Bureau of Education in Washington, D.C., was elected superintendent of the Dallas Public School System. He came to Dallas and joined the First Baptist Church. Criswell saw his opportunity. He met with Dr. Estes and told him what he had been trying to do. Dr. Estes said, "It will be a tragedy if education ever becomes the sole responsibility of the state. If that ever happens totalitarianism and a dictatorship is just around the corner. I will help you. I will help you launch the school."[16]

At the next deacons' meeting Dr. Estes explained the value of the church school to them. When he finished, the leading deacon, who had opposed the school in earlier days, stood up and said, "I have opposed this in all these years past but I have changed my mind. I would now like to vote in favor of our establishing the school."[17]

The school officially began with 125 students at the start of the school year in the fall of 1972. Criswell had struggled for more than thirty-five years to get the school off the ground. His dream had now become a reality because of his tenacity. When Criswell sets his mind to a task, it is almost always accomplished.

The First Baptist Academy has expanded rapidly over the years. It now houses two campuses, one downtown for grades K–12, and one called the "East Campus" for grades K–6. Total enrollment approaches the one thousand mark. Many of the families who have children in the Academy eventually find their way into the membership of the First Baptist Church through the activities of the school.

Criswell's philosophy of education for the Academy is deeply rooted in the basic fundamental tenets of the Christian faith. It is his desire that a top quality education be provided. However, at the center of this education is an emphasis on a genuine belief in the Bible:

> Not everybody would want to go to a school like this. And it's not made for everybody. This is made for people who would love to give their child a Christian education, and I mean *emphatically* Christian. And I don't mean liberal Christianity. I mean fundamental, conservative Christianity. Teaching them that the Bible is true. *Never* is that parabolic. By that I mean that the Garden of Eden is not a myth. There was a Garden of Eden. Adam and Eve are not fabled characters; they are actual characters. The story of Noah and the Ark is not a moral tale. It is something that happened in God's providence. Now, that's the way I believe the Bible, and that's the way the school will be taught.[18]

Criswell would like to see many suburban Christian schools started and sponsored by the downtown church with all of them feeding high school students to the downtown facility. But Criswell is over eighty years of age, and some of his dreams will ultimately be left to future leadership.

Because Criswell was so well educated himself and because he had seen the doors of opportunity that have been opened for him due to advanced degrees, he believes a good education is essential. I once heard Criswell tell one of my own daughters that the two keys to life were to love Jesus and to study hard in school.

> The pastor's Ph.D. degree is more than a wall decoration. It is the insignia of a scholar who spends every day in study, not only in his specialty but of the larger world

> as well. Dr. Criswell has his study time at home rather than at the church in order to conserve time. A spacious wing was added to the parsonage to house Criswell's large library, desk, work tables, and filing cabinets, with a well appointed reception room. Books line his walls, and a separate large room has library type stacks filled with books on every conceivable subject. Criswell feels keenly that the early morning hours when the mind is fresh, should be used for study.[19]

Criswell loves to study. He had even mentioned at times that he would have made an "ideal monk."[20] His desire for exactness often causes him to overstate his case. The casual listener probably believes most everything Criswell says because of his impeccable reputation. Yet Criswell strives to document each point. This characteristic dates back to 1937, to his doctoral dissertation at the Southern Baptist Theological Seminary. Criswell's use of footnotes was so extensive that he actually apologized for their multiplied use in the Foreword of his dissertation: "The footnotes may seem excessive in number, but I have sought to make possible a verification for every conclusion established, and the means by which the conclusion was drawn."[21] An excellent example of Criswell's scholarly writing may be seen in Appendix G where Criswell reviews *The Southern Baptist Holy War*, written by Joe Edward Barnhart, professor at the University of North Texas.

Criswell Bible Institute

Because of Criswell's love for education, he wanted to start a Bible Institute for the membership of the church.

> I began to look at these people who work in our churches and how most of them are without training. They don't have any training at all. Here is a wonderful busi-

> nessman and he is successful out there, but he does not know anything about the Bible or about the church or about church members. He is just without knowledge. Well, if you could get the fellow and teach him, it would be an untold blessing to him.[22]

Criswell thought the Institute would begin with about thirty students. He remembered that Baylor University had started with only about twenty students. To Criswell's amazement more than 440 people showed up the first night to register for class. People had come from Oklahoma, south Texas, and east Texas. Professors were enlisted from Southwestern Baptist Theological Seminary in nearby Fort Worth, Dallas Baptist University, and Dallas Theological Seminary. The second semester over 550 enrolled. The classes met on Sunday and Tuesday evenings. Criswell saw that he had provided an answer to an evidently pressing need.

Leo Eddleman, Baptist scholar and educator, was asked to be president of the Institute, which was fast becoming a school. He immediately began to work toward accreditation with the Southern Association of Schools and Colleges. Criswell did not see the school as competitive with other Baptist denominational schools. But others did:

> There were some professors at Southwestern Seminary who were highly critical of what we did. Oh, they were very vocal in it and critical—just some of them. And then across the convention there were editors who took potshots at it in their editorial columns, but after we wrote to them and explained to them what it was we were doing, those same editors wrote words of commendation for us. And the same thing about the Seminary—when we talked to Dr. Naylor and told him what we were trying to do, why, Dr. Naylor could see that there was no fear of any rival or competitive group in what we were trying to do.[23]

So with wounds healed the infant school continued to grow. Criswell wanted to help people further their education:

> If we had a Bible Institute in West Texas, one in East Texas, one in South Texas, and this one in North Texas, it would help us all great deal. There are many, many, many preachers who do not go to the seminary for many reasons. . . . And you need a trained laity far more than we now have, and a Bible Institute would help fill that need.[24]

The dedication of the Criswell Bible Institute took place in January 1971. The school was dedicated to teaching the entire Bible as the infallible, inerrant Word of God and to the task of deepening the lives of lay people and vocational Christian leaders. Criswell did not particularly like their using his name, but allowed them to in order to identify the school with conservative, evangelical Christianity:

> The reason that they use that word "Criswell" in the name . . . is to announce to the world the type of theology to be expected here. And of course the articles of faith will work to implement that theological position. Now, I inveighed against the use of my name. I still don't like it; I don't like for them to call it the Criswell Bible College. . . . But they said they wanted to do that in order for the world to know the kind of teaching that was going to be taught here, and they said, "You are identified with the inspiration of the Bible and the belief in the supernatural, the deity of Christ, the virgin birth of the Lord, the resurrection, the return of Christ; you're identified with those things and when you put that name on the institute, immediately it defines the kind of theological teaching that we are to expect."[25]

In early 1975, Paige Patterson came to serve as the school's second president. Dr. Eddleman was getting older, and the demand for a younger, energetic man was necessary. Under Patterson's capable leadership the school has made great strides in growth and has developed a reputation as a valid academic institution. The lay institute expanded from simply a night school to a full-time day school on the college level. The name of the school was changed to the Criswell Center for Biblical Studies. This umbrella title would oversee the many ministries of the school's operation. The school has become an outstanding training ground for ministerial students and others called of God into Christian service. As the fully accredited Bible College and graduate school expanded, offering a variety of degree programs, the Southern Association recommended that the school simply be called Criswell College, by which it is now known.

Time has proven Criswell true to his word. Criswell College is simply another school from which many of the students in the Baptist denomination choose. Pressure is not applied to attend Criswell College. The students from First Baptist Church, Dallas, attend a variety of other Baptist schools, including Baylor University, Hardin-Simmons, and Howard Payne, as well as many secular universities.

At the beginning of each school year, all the faculty members of Criswell College sign the doctrinal statement of faith, thus ensuring the future of the school's theological position. An endowment fund has been set up to help the school every year as long as the mission purpose and biblical belief remain true to Criswell's intent. Otherwise all financial support from the fund will be cut off.

For many years, Criswell wanted a radio station affiliated with the church and school. Under Patterson's tenure his dream became a reality. In May 1976, KCBI-FM signed on the air as the broadcast arm of the Criswell Center for Biblical Studies. The listening audience has continued to respond very favorably to this twenty-four-hour Christian voice. The station has a 50,000 watt international shortwave station to reach central Europe and South America as well. In recent days, the radio station has expanded to 100,000 watts, placing it in the category of one of the most powerful stations in the country.

School of the Prophets

Criswell wants his influence to pass on to future generations. This is not out of desire for personal glory or fame but rather out of love for conservative theology and hatred for liberal theology. Therefore, a yearly one week seminar on church dynamics was begun in 1971. This seminar came to be called "The School of the Prophets." Criswell said the school's name went back to the days of Samuel, when there were schools of prophets in ancient Bible times in Israel. In these schools, an older, more experienced prophet taught younger men what he knew about the Lord.

Criswell also notes that the biblical phrase "take my yoke upon you" (Matthew 11:29), could better be translated "enroll in my school." Criswell, therefore, believes it is important for other ministers to have full review of the work in Dallas in order to see what has effectively worked. These pastors take many ideas back to their home churches and try to implement them in a way best suited for their own particular situation. Criswell admits that everything done in the Dallas church will not work in exactly the same way at other churches, but he emphasizes that God will bless a man if he gives himself totally to the Lord and to the work of the ministry.

It is during the School of the Prophets that Criswell's ideas and philosophies are most often revealed. This is partially true because of the environment. All these young preachers have traveled to Dallas to hear how their "hero," W. A. Criswell, planned and accomplished his goals. There is even one session each year called "The Lion's Den," when any question on any topic may be asked. The visiting ministers often ask intriguing questions many of the church members or staff would be fearful of. The visiting ministers will be gone in a few days and are not threatened by the situation. But "The Lion's Den" session is also visited by many church members.

Criswell emphasizes several key points during the School of the Prophets. He encourages every man to devote himself each morning to the study of the Bible. Criswell gets up early, puts on some old clothes, and studies until noon. He does not have to be fresh of mind to shave, comb his hair, or put on his shoes. He believes a lot of preachers waste early morning time putting on their clothes when they could be using their most alert moments of the day for God.

> When I began my first full time pastorate out of the seminary, the deacons in that town said to me, "Now our pastor before you, your predecessor, had his study here at the church. He was a wise man in the 18 years and we think it would be good for you to have your study at the church." Not knowing, I took my little library, . . . and I had my study at the church. It didn't take me but one day to find out. . . . Anybody would say, "We're not going to take up his time—we just want to say 'hello' to him," and they would come in and take 30 and 45 minutes telling me hello. That went on all the time. So I gathered myself up and all of my belongings and I took them out to the parsonage. . . . And from that day until this my study is in the place where I live. And I announced to the church . . ."My morning is for God. In the afternoon I'll do any work that the church demands. In the evening I'll go to any service, but in the morning I want to be left alone with God. Don't call me . . . don't telephone me . . . don't come to see me . . . don't ask me

> . . . don't look at me. Leave me alone. In the morning I want to be with God." And when you do that and you stand up in the pulpit, the people will know that you have been with the Lord. It will be apparent. It will be the most manifestly publicly publicized thing in all your life. "It is apparent this preacher of ours has been with God." Do that! Do that![26]

Criswell often talks about the future of the Southern Baptist denomination at the School of the Prophets. Since he has been one of the leading workers in the Convention and his church a heavy contributor, he has earned the right to be heard. Although optimistic at present, he believes the Convention is headed for trouble. He notes that every conservative work, whether school or church, sooner or later becomes liberal. He often cites Harvard, which was once a conservative theological institution but is now liberal, as an example.

Criswell warns the young preacher to be careful regarding the intimate details of anyone's life. If he listens to every sin a member commits, every time he preaches on that topic the member will think he is talking only to him. The minister should be a friend and a source of hope and encouragement to his people regardless of what they have done. Because of Criswell's sixty years of experience in the pastorate he usually has good advice for the convocation. The typical School of the Prophets has been accurately summarized by B. Keith:

> They listened intently to Criswell devouring every word, like young executives pouring over the stockmarket reports, or doctors at a medical convention hearing of the latest developments in medical science. Excited young men, optimistic, sincere, they were convinced Criswell was a prophet of God and through him they expected to find some of the answers to the perplexing problems facing today's ministers.[27]

Criswell advises the ministers to speak without notes. A man who preaches without notes must prepare more than one who uses notes, he believes. Although Criswell does not write out his sermons, he does outline them in detail. "I outline my sermons extensively and write a good deal under each point. I have always preached by outline. Do today. I never take the outline into the pulpit, but I have it and follow it in my mind."[28] He admits that he has had strange psychological feelings about it:

> Sometimes I sit there and the choir is singing before I preach and the whole sermon will leave me and I'm blank. The mind is one of the strangest psychological instruments you ever saw in your life. Sometimes I'll be there and have the points going through my mind and I'll think of the first one and the last one and the three middle ones just disappear from my mind. You just keep firing away and it will come back to you. If I trust my memory, in the goodness of God, it will not let me down.[29]

Although Criswell does not manuscript his sermons verbatim, many of them are transcribed from cassette tape, then adapted for reading. Criswell has had fifty-one books published. Most have been distributed by major book publishers. Several of his works have made a profound impact on the pulpits and pews of the world. (For a complete listing of Criswell's written works, see Appendix F.)

Criswell has never lost his love for studying and learning. He has found a variety of ways to communicate his sermons over the years. He presents them in a manner that is exegetical, textual, topical, making a study of the life of a Bible character, or presenting an exposition (verse by verse study) through an entire book of the Bible. The latter has probably become his favorite because if he does not finish his sermon the following week he can start where he left off.

Yet Criswell would be the first to admit that the key to ministerial success was not found in simply intellectual pursuits or learned accomplishments. Faith and courage in God should always be the source of the pastor's strength. Criswell often warns the young preacher not to resort to speaking on old news and contemporary subjects of the day, "hashed and rehashed" on radio and television:

> I don't blame people for not going to those churches and those who go yawn and go to sleep or go play golf the next Sunday. The reason we go to church is to find out: Does God say anything? We know what all the economists and other folks say.[30]

Criswell further states that the preacher may not even be as capable as the news reporter, economist, or analyst, and if all he does is review their news, the man in the pew will quit coming:

> When he goes up there to church and that preacher, who usually is about half as capable as the other men, rehashes the same thing, he doesn't go back so the church dies, the denomination dies, the school dies, the mission board dies, everything dies. What the man wants to know when he goes to church is: Does God say anything? Well, if he does, what does God say? You've got it there in the book. What does he say? And that's what the preacher does and when the preacher will do that the layman will sit there and listen to him. . . . And he'll come back, . . . and he'll bring his children and he'll get converted and he'll get baptized.[31]

Criswell always encourages the young preacher to be himself: "You may be a fine imitation of someone else, but listen, you're the best example of you in this entire world. There's nobody like you, so be yourself."[32]

Praise Service

Perhaps the most important part of the entire church program, other than Criswell's preaching, occurs at the end of the service. The invitation is extended to come to the Lord or to join the church. It is beautifully spoken by Criswell: "And that's our invitation to you—Come; from the lower floor, from the balcony round and down these stairwells on either side—come; a couple, you, a family, you, or just one somebody you, come!" (To Criswell, any response a person makes is a good response. This is because coming down the aisle, to Criswell, is equated to responding to God, and responding to God is always right.) After an invitation has been given and people have responded by coming forward to join the church or make some other decision, Criswell has a "praise service":

> When people come to the altar, praise God and rejoice. If they have family members present, get them down there or their friends, let them stand with them. Everytime someone comes down front and stands up for Jesus, it blesses him and the entire congregation. I can't name the number of times we've had people side by side stretched all across this auditorium, three times a day on Sunday. We always make a lot of the people who come.[33]

The congregation responds well to Criswell during this time. He laughs, cries, prays, praises, and usually goes on and on over the decision the person has made. Comments will be made to the individuals that build them up and immediately make them feel warmly welcomed into the church family:

"What do you do here in the city?"

"Well . . . you're going to be rich!"

"My, what a beautiful family."

"Thank you for wearing that red dress. . . . I love a red dress!"

"We love having you here being part of us."

"How precious is this moment before God and His dear people here at First Baptist Church."

"We are going to heaven from here . . . and if you're not here you might miss it!"

"You can't get into the kingdom without shaking my hand!"

Since Criswell has been the pastor for more than forty-three years, he is usually acquainted with a relative of nearly everyone who comes forward. Often he will tell a story or relive an experience with a family member. Naturally, if the family member is present, he will be publicly called forward to stand beside the person. If it is a child who has made a decision before the Lord, Criswell will place the child between the parents to emphasize the whole family. It is one of the most special times in the life of the church. Many believe it has been a key factor in Criswell's success.

It was mentioned earlier that when Criswell made his public declaration to be a preacher, it was hardly noticed because of the older man who made the same decision in that service. The older man seemed to be given the "spotlight" on that occasion. Even as a child Criswell felt the sting of unimportance. Because of that experience Criswell goes out of his way to welcome children for any and every decision they make for God.

Because Criswell believes that the New Testament presupposes a mature mind (i.e., one can read and understand the Scripture) he does not push early childhood conversions or baptisms. However, he would never, never discourage a child from making a decision for the Lord. Therefore, years ago Criswell devised the scenario known as "step toward God." This means that although the child may be too young to fully comprehend all the tenets of the Christian faith, he or she may still feel a love and devotion to God.

Therefore, his decision is publicly recognized by the church. The child experiences love and acceptance by the church and can continue to grow into a fuller understanding of the Christian faith as time passes. Criswell has written a small booklet entitled "Joining the Church." It is designed for children to help them in this process (see Appendix H).

Criswell has also developed a plan whereby seminary or Bible college students can join First Baptist Church yet remain on their home church roles in order not to lose their home church mission support.This is called joining by "watchcare." The church will spiritually watch and care for the student while he or she is in the Dallas area. This reveals the repercussions in Criswell's heart from his own experiences while growing up—he tries to help anyone who is seeking to do God's work. The nature of the service can be summed up in the following words:

> Criswell seems totally uninhibited. He says what he thinks and does what he sees the situation as calling for, whether it is taking a child up in his arms for a visit or verbally scolding his opponents. . . . The fact that a thing "isn't done" bothers him not at all! For example, Dr. Criswell often breaks out singing in the midst of his sermon singing either a hymn or some popular number to illustrate his message. The people love him for it, although many of them recognize that his enthusiasm exceeds his singing ability! Such things may seem unconventional, but when Criswell does them, somehow they seem the thing to do.[34]

Outreach

Criswell is not afraid to admit his failures or misgivings about other people to his fellow ministers. He uses his failures to encourage others not to make the same mistakes. Criswell relates a story regarding a friend he met during his student days at Baylor, whom Criswell thought the most unpromising preacher in the university:

> I looked at him one day and said to myself, "I think God made a mistake. Not in a thousand years would I call that fellow to be a preacher." . . . Well, we went through Baylor and then seminary and the clouds of war gathered, and the War Department asked for men to serve as chaplains and that boy answered the call and immediately went overseas.
>
> He stayed with his fighting units all through the war and never returned home until the war was over and he was the most decorated chaplain in the armies of the United States. Again and again he was wounded but he stayed with his men.
>
> One day after the war was over I was walking down the street during the Southern Baptist convention, and I met that friend face-to-face and he was in the uniform of his country. And when I looked at him—the man I had held in such contempt—I was overwhelmed with unworthiness and shame and bowed my head to God and asked forgiveness.
>
> God could see that chaplain ministering to all those dying boys on the battlefield and called him to be His man.
>
> Sometimes it does us good to admit that God know a lot more than we do.[35]

When an unusual situation occurs in the life of Criswell, he often looks beyond the incident for a deeper, more profound meaning. Since Criswell believes that God is sovereign (in charge of the affairs of life) there are no mistakes or surprises in our lives that God has not previously reviewed. Therefore, it is our responsibility to learn and grow in each situation.

> One morning he arrived at the church quite early—which he seldom does since he studies at home—and as he walked down Patterson Street he saw a large crowd of people gathered at the corner right in front of the church. He elbowed his way into the crowd to see what was happening and saw there on the steps a man in workingman's clothes, with his hands over his back reaching toward the front door of the church. As the pastor looked down into the man's face he breathed his last breath.
>
> "And the man died there on our front doorstep with his hands over his head reaching toward our church," the pastor recalled.
>
> The ambulance came and took the body away, the police dispersed the crowd, and they probably soon forgot about the incident, but it remained in the pastor's mind.
>
> "Who was he? What was he doing at our church door and just at the hour I was to arrive?" the pastor kept asking himself. "Was he saved? Well, that was the beginning of our mission program in the church—to reach the people downtown, the rich, the poor, the workingman."
>
> He immediately went before the deacons and asked for the money to start three missions.[36]

The mission outreach of the church has grown to include twenty-six chapels. (For a complete listing of the chapels and information regarding the mission work, see Appendix I.) Each year a large percentage of the church budget is designated to the mission work.

Criswell is never bothered by the interruptions the "street people" sometimes cause. One Sunday morning an intoxicated man came into the service, walked up to the front of the church, and began to shout at Criswell. Several men quickly "helped" the man out the door.

Criswell stopped, waited patiently until the man left, then calmly replied, "That is just one of the many privileges of being the pastor of a downtown church!" The congregation broke out in laughter and applause.

Notes

1. Louis McBeth, *The First Baptist Church of Dallas* (Grand Rapids: Zondervan, 1968), pp. 282-83.
2. Ibid., p. 283.
3. Ibid.
4. Ibid., p. 288.
5. W. A. Criswell, "Walking by Faith Alone," sermon preached at First Baptist Church, 31 August 1986.
6. T. Charlton and R. Spain, *Oral Memoirs of W. A. Criswell* (Waco, Tex.: Baylor Univ., 1973), p. 192.
7. Ibid., p. 226.
8. Charlton and Spain, *Oral Memoirs*, p. 192.
9. Ibid., pp. 229-32.
10. Ibid., pp. 261-62.
11. Ibid., p. 263.
12. W. A. Criswell, "The Church of the Open Door," sermon preached at First Baptist Church, 9 July 1968.
13. Charlton and Spain, *Oral Memoirs*, p. 209.
14. Ibid., pp. 209-10.
15. Ibid., p. 211.
16. Ibid., p. 212.
17. Ibid.
18. Ibid., p. 207.
19. McBeth, *The First Baptist Church of Dallas*, pp. 326-27.
20. Charlton and Spain, *Oral Memoirs*, p. 122.
21. W. A. Criswell, *The John the Baptist Movement in Its Relation to the Christian Movement* (doctoral diss., Southern Baptist Theological Seminary, 1937), p. v.
22. Charlton and Spain, *Oral Memoirs*, p. 195.
23. Ibid., pp. 199-200.
24. Ibid., p. 194.
25. Ibid., pp. 197-98.
26. W. A. Criswell, "Founder's Day Message," sermon preached at First Baptist Church, 29 September 1987.

27. B. Keith, *W. A. Criswell: The Authorized Biography* (Old Tappan, N. J.: Revell, 1973), p. 173.
28. Charlton and Spain, *Oral Memiors*, p. 149.
29. Keith, *W. A. Criswell*, p. 160.
30. Ibid., pp. 162-63.
31. Charlton and Spain, *Oral Memoirs*, p. 237.
32. Keith, *W. A. Criswell*, p. 163.
33. Ibid., p. 165.
34. McBeth, *The First Baptist Church of Dallas*, p. 326.
35. Keith, *W. A. Criswell*, p. 170.
36. Ibid., p. 166.

7
Pastor

Criswell loves being part of a downtown church. Although he was raised poor and pastored country churches in his youth, he has found his love in the city.

> I don't like a suburban church. I like a downtown First Baptist Church that just has everybody in it—black and white, pea-green and purple, rich and poor, crazy, nuts, screwballs, wise, professors, smart . . . you know just everybody, and I like that.[1]

Criswell believes the greatest preacher who ever lived was Charles Haddon Spurgeon. Spurgeon preached in England during the nineteenth century. Pictures and busts of Spurgeon decorate Criswell's study at his home. Spurgeon preached in the heart of a large downtown area. It is only fitting that Criswell would want to emulate such a worthy example.

> One day on the street I met a wonderful man who has an office in one of those tall buildings that look down upon the city, casting a shadow over our church when the sun rises in the east. He said to me, "I cannot tell you how it affects me when I look out the window of my office and see children on that playground in the heart

of the city. It is like nothing I have ever seen in the world." I feel exactly like that fine businessman. How glorious to see children on the church playground gathered in the name of the Lord. It is a wonderful thing that, amid these skyscrapers and within the teeming life of the insurance, banking, merchandising, wholesaling, and the rest of those businesses and companies that contribute to the intense life of the queenly city of Dallas that is its heart, we also have a lighthouse shining for God.[2]

Criswell does not like to think of himself as an influence in denominational life. He is more interested in the life and activity of the church he so faithfully pastors. This point cannot be overstressed: Criswell's philosophy of ministry centers on activity and involvement. Where there is no activity or involvement, there is a dead church.

I am so wrapped up in what I am doing—I am preparing a sermon; I am getting a bunch of men going; we're building a building; we're launching a school; we're building an institute; we're having a revival; we're praying for the lost—I am so caught up in what I'm doing that I never think about those other things.[3]

One might think that a man of Criswell's stature and influence could possibly be looking for a way to further his career or reputation, but not Criswell. His love is the First Baptist Church in Dallas:

I have no interest in anything except furthering the Kingdom of God through the First Baptist Church in Dallas. I don't want to be the president of anything. To show you how disinterested I am, there is a . . . very old and famous four-year senior Baptist college—one of the finest we have in the world. While I was over there one time, they asked me to be the president of that school. And they said, "You don't give us an answer now. You

> pray about this for two weeks, and at such and such a day at such and such hour we'll call you and you give us your answer." So, the chairman of that committee called me, and I had no idea what he was talking about. . . . Finally it came back to my mind—why, that man is the chairman of that committee who is getting a president for that college and at this hour I was to tell them my decision! I had forgotten about it altogether; it hadn't stayed in my mind thirty minutes.[4]

Criswell does not keep this to himself. He constantly reaffirms to his flock that they are his people. Although the church is large, it is extremely warm and friendly, after the example of its pastor.

> Though he has prayed with presidents, served as the head of the Southern Baptist Convention and is often recognized in public, Criswell brushes aside the notion that he is a celebrity or even a denominational leader. He insists he is "still a country pastor." "I don't think I am a celebrity," he says. "I just don't. I never think about it. I'm just the pastor of this church, that's all. Nothing more. . . . I am so consumed in my pastoral work that I don't think of those things."[5]

Criswell can say whatever he wishes, but the fact remains the same. *He* is the drawing card, the central figure in the life of the church:

> These are valid explanations of First Baptist Church growth, but they are all secondary. Actually, one man stands behind this growth—Wallie Amos Criswell. His powerful preaching, his dynamic personality, his unerring leadership, and his public image as a representative of the best of the old time religion make Criswell a dynamic Dallas figure. The blunt truth is that hundreds of people come to the First Baptist Church to hear Criswell. The attendance declines noticeably when it is known he will be absent. Members have great affection

> for the man, with almost unbelievable confidence in his preaching and his judgment about church policies. The pastor has fully justified both their affection and confidence. Because he is sometimes controversial, Criswell probably does not enjoy the universal esteem of the larger Dallas community. However, no man in the history of First Baptist Church has stood taller with his own people.[6]

On Criswell's fortieth anniversary as pastor of First Baptist Church, the church gave him a new Mercedes. In addition to many accolades during the day, a moving, gripping slide production was presented (see Appendix J). All who saw the presentation felt that it depicted the life and ministry of W. A. Criswell in an excellent manner.

Criswell has a flair for the "dramatic." He not only speaks, he entertains. He uses this to capture his audience, to drive a point home much the same way an entertainer does. Criswell knows people are not interested in dull lectures, and his audience stays alert as he speaks.

In 1973 Criswell predicted, "Within ten years there will be over 25,000 members in the church. On a good Sunday we will have over 10,000 in Sunday School and our yearly budget will go beyond $8,000,000.00 a year."[7] Criswell was almost exactly right concerning the membership and budget, and not far off on the attendance figures (see Appendix C).

Oddly enough, Criswell's associates fear going outside the standard accepted way of doing things. They do not like the dramatic. Occasionally a staff member will do something publicly at a service that the church really enjoys. No one enjoys it more than Criswell. But if you are too unorthodox, you could end your own career.

Criswell is conservative in nearly every area of his life. He does not try to associate or cooperate with those of the liberal persuasion because he has found over the years that it does not do any good:

> To a liberal I am anathema. It's like one of those men at Nashville, Tennessee, one of our denominational executives. He said to me, "Now, don't try to placate the liberals; they're not going to like you no matter what you say or what you do. So you just go on being yourself and let that fall to any level it may descend." Well, I've never forgotten that. I don't try to placate any liberal. He's not going to like me; I don't care what I say or do. So I just don't try it.[8]

The Active Pastor

The church facilities have continued to grow over the years. Since 1970 the following buildings were either acquired or built to enable the downtown facility to comfortably house over 12,000 people during the morning services: KCBI Building (Reilly Building), 1970; Christian Education Building, 1973; Easterwood Building, 1976 (now sold to Lincoln properties); Ross Avenue Parking Garage, 1980; "Mary C" Building (donated by the late multi-millionaire Mary Crowley), 1983; skywalk access between "Spurgeon" Harris and the Christian Education Building, 1983; the Ruth Ray Hunt Youth Building (donated by Mrs. H. L. Hunt), 1986; and the 505 Building, 1989.

There is one major goal Criswell still desires for the church. For many years he has wanted to build a large dining facility where the church family could assemble for meetings and to eat together. Coleman Hall, the present facility, has long since lost that kind of capacity. The church has owned a piece of property for some time, which formerly housed Radio Station KCBI-FM and now houses the college Sunday school ministry. The property is on the corner of St. Paul and Old San Jacinto. More than twenty years ago, McBeth wrote in his centennial history work, *The First Baptist Church of Dallas*, that "plans are being tentatively projected to build here a structure to match and connect with the Criswell Building. It will contain kitchens, a dining and fellowship center, and educational space."[9] In his oral memoirs, recorded in 1973, Criswell assured Charlton and Spain that the building would soon be under construction:

> Spain: And this is then in the final stages of planning it.
> Criswell: Yes.
> Spain: And will definitely be a reality.
> Criswell: Yes. They have a picture of it and everything. It's all ready.[10]

As of this writing the building of the facility has not begun, nor are there plans to do so.

Criswell has often spoken of his fear that the old sanctuary could burn to the ground and while it was being rebuilt the people would have no large facility in which to meet. He believes that this could cause a lot of families to begin attending local suburban churches and that the downtown church would not survive. Oddly enough, there is little talk regarding such a possibility among the congregation. If anything, during such a crisis the people who have faithfully followed Criswell over the years would no doubt want to rally around their pastor, rise up, and build.

Criswell is often frustrated because of his lack of patience in administrative duties. He hates details, which he feels often cause programs and plans to fail in any organization. Therefore, he deals with problems on a broad scale rather than in a specific manner.

For example, in April of 1984, Criswell was disgusted with some of the staff for their lack of support in their attendance in the worship services of the church. In a letter to each individual staff member he wrote:

It is unthinkable and unimaginable to me that our staff leadership does not attend the services of the church every time the door is open. However other things may be in organizational life, the church service is the heartbeat of everything Christianity is about. . . .

Search your own soul. Do you faithfully attend the services of the church? Search your own heart. How long has it been since you came down to the front with a soul you had won to the Lord, or a family you had won to the church? Honestly and truly, I tell you an ugly and harsh fact. It seems to me that out of all the people in the church some of our staff take the smallest and littlest and paltriest interest in it. I am sure that you are there more often than I think, but I tell you another fact. There are some of you that I do not see in attendance in the church for months at a time.

Let me suggest that you do something. You get to yourself, and you pray through your commitment to Christ and to the work we are trying to do here in the First Baptist Church of Dallas. If you find that your interests are in some other area, let me strongly suggest that you go to that area and work, and leave your place open for us here in the church to find somebody who will love God enough to attend the services and to try to win people to the Lord.

Through the years . . . I have hoped and prayed that God would change our staff, but I have given up that hope. It has come down to the place where it is as simple as this: We are going to have a staff that loves the Lord, serves the Lord, is present upon the services of the Lord, wins people to Christ, comes forward with them at the services of the church; or else, we are going to start all over again with a prayer that God will send us somebody else.

You think this through. You pray this through. And you make the decision what you feel led to do.

Your frustrated, disappointed and heartbroken pastor, W. A. Criswell[11]

In the fourth paragraph of the letter, Criswell refers to only "several of our staff." Yet each individual staff member received a personal letter addressed to him. Some who had been working hard, attending the meetings, and actively involved in the work of the church felt unnecessarily rebuked.

The old axiom regarding employer-employee relations is "Praise publicly, rebuke privately." Criswell's view seems to be "Praise publicly, rebuke publicly." As imperfect as he may be in his administrative skills, he is still in charge.

> Dr. Criswell . . . prefers preaching and shepherding the flock to the business and administrative work of the church. Any institution that large, and with that income, requires skillful administration. Not that Criswell is inept—all who know him marvel at his organizational skill. Close observers credit a large part of the church growth since 1944 to his brilliant organizational ability. As an administrator he has the ability to inspire confidence, to know exactly where he is going, and to enlist the hearty cooperation of others. Yet, the pastor finds such mundane details tiring, so the church has wisely enlisted a corps of administrative helpers. When things are going well, the pastor may appear at his office at the church only rarely, and then not stay for long. His study is at home, and he receives some visitors there. However, the outsider who thinks Criswell has largely withdrawn from the actual running of the church is both right and wrong. He has turned the day-to-day work over to others. But the guiding genius behind the entire massive machinery is still W. A. Criswell, and no one else.[12]

Criswell does not simply cater to those who are intelligent or wealthy. He has a heart filled with compassion for those less fortunate. As early as 1962 a Special Education Department was begun to provide a place for Bible instruction and ministry to children with special needs and learning disabilities. The ministry has continued to grow. It now accommodates both adults and children. Today this ministry is in the capable hands of Miss Libby Reynolds, an employee of the church for thirty years.

Criswell seemingly has a love for everybody, even his opponents. His positive outlook on life makes him respected by all. The Dallas newspapers have written many articles about him. None, however, was more impressive than the "High Profile" that appeared in the *Dallas Morning News*. (For a portion of this article, see Appendix K.)

Criswell has kept the fires of activity going strong for more than forty years at the church in Dallas. Activity and involvement have resulted in growth and production. From the outset of his ministry, he communicated optimism, enthusiasm, and activity:

> Nothing is more characteristic of Criswell than his bubbling enthusiasm. He is optimistic and effervescent. His face is often wreathed in a big, friendly smile. He likes to give every task his best, and he expects the same of those around him. In 1948 he wrote that he would be flying from Memphis to Dallas on a big airliner in only an hour and fifty-five minutes! He added, "I like those big planes that really get up and go. I like big churches that do the same!"[13]

Every time things get calm, Criswell gets uneasy. He does not like to let up or take, as the Bible refers to it, an "ease in Zion" (Amos 6:1). Every day is a challenge and an opportunity for growth and expansion.

> We have a tremendous program here during the week. We have this recreational program that goes on all the time and that's an extensive one. We have, the Lord only knows, how many luncheons and dinners down here in the days of the week. The kitchen is booked solidly. If you want to go over there and do something for the next year, you'll have trouble. It is used all the time. There are

> people that meet down here all the time. We have this grade school going down there in the weekday, and that carries the kindergarten with it and the day nursery. And we have our Bible Institute, and then we have the endless meetings; of missionary groups like the women, conversational English classes for the foreigners who come into the city—it's a way for us to reach them—and the many, many meetings of the church that are entailed in its organized life. There is something going on here all the time, day and night.[14]

To Criswell, all that activity is a way of revealing the life and vitality taking place within the church. Without it the church would simply become a historical landmark. He is probably correct. On any given Sunday night a lot of activity and good preaching is taking place at First Baptist Church. While all the other churches in the downtown area are closed, First Baptist is thriving and growing.

Criswell firmly believes that the reason God has blessed him over the years is because he has remained faithful in preaching the Bible. God has not promised to bless every program or activity in which we participate, but He has promised to bless His Word:

> There's no such thing as saying, "This part of the Bible is not true," then expecting all the rest of it to be acceptable as true from then on. What happens to you is, when you refuse this part, it's not long until you start refusing this part and then this part and this part and finally it becomes nothing but a piece of antique literature, riddled and decimated, destroyed and shattered by unbelief. You leave it a shambles. The man that doesn't believe in the authenticity of the record in Genesis will not believe in the authenticity of the record in Daniel. Then the man that doesn't believe in Daniel won't believe in Jonah, and the man that doesn't believe in Jonah won't believe the miracles of the New Testament. And the man that doesn't believe in the New Testament will not

> believe in the virgin birth of Christ. The man that doesn't believe in the virgin birth of Christ will come to where he doesn't believe in the bodily resurrection. And it goes on and on and on. The Bible is *one book*. And if I come to the place where I don't believe parts of it, I eventually come to the place where I look upon it as you would Aesop's Fables. It has moral tales and that's all. Has no authority.[15]

For W. A. Criswell, that would be unthinkable.

The Teaching Pastor

Criswell's educational philosophies have contributed to his church and to the Southern Baptist Convention in many ways. Here are seventeen of them.

DELEGATION

Truett did the work of ten men. Criswell would rather hire ten men to do the work, thus freeing himself to have time to build the church. Criswell instilled the educational philosophy of "recruitment" into the programming of the church. Today every division constantly recruits new workers, thus expanding its areas of ministry and freeing up the leader to expand the division. In this first contribution, Criswell changed the direction of the educational programming of the church by spreading the work out and letting other people help. "Let the pastor take that dedicated group [staff] into his confidence. They will help achieve his every goal and work with him to bring his every dream to realization."[16]

Criswell's view of the First Baptist Church is hardly modest. He believes that the church and its ministries are the best in the world. Even though the church is located in downtown Dallas, thus presenting a hardship on some families who must travel many miles, Criswell believes the trip is worth the effort. I have often heard Criswell make the following analogy: "If you or your child were sick, you would not go to just any doctor. You would find the very best doctor in town. If you discovered the doctor's office was on the other side of town, you would gladly drive the distance because you knew you would be receiving the very best attention possible. Well, that is why we want you to come join our church. We want to give you and your family the best spiritual care possible." Criswell believes that the church ought to achieve excellence in Christian ministry. It is important to strive to be the best in every endeavor for the Lord. In a day when many Christian organizations are faltering, it is admirable to see a man and his ministry as a credit, rather than a "blot," to the cause of Christ.

FAMILY FIRST

Criswell's educational philosophy always included putting his personal devotion to the ministry as top priority in his life. In recent years he has changed his mind on that issue.

> I have a confession to make. All through the years . . . of my life I have placed my ministry first. There has been no exception to that, any day, any night. I have placed my work as a preacher and as a pastor first. A thousand times am I asked in these preacher conferences, "If you have your life to do over again, is there anything you would change?" And I am beginning to reply, "There is. If I had my life to live over again, I would place my family first and my ministry second." This is God's charge, this is God's calling first under His gracious and loving hands to have a Christian Home, to rear our children in the love and nurture of the Lord and the other things in life will take their place under the hand and choice, under the supervision and surveillance of the great Almighty God.[17]

Thus, we see Criswell's desire to help other ministers learn from his mistakes.

HARD WORK

Criswell believes you should be hard on yourself. If you work hard (which he demands of his staff) life will be easier for you. But if you are easy on yourself, life will be hard on you. Criswell is harder on himself than any opponent ever tried to be. This part of Criswell's education philosophy could be stated, "Hate failure and work hard to avoid it." He often laments that he has not accomplished more in his lifetime. This may sound odd since he has done so much to help shape evangelical Christianity in America today, not to mention downtown Dallas. (The church now owns six city blocks.)

But one must remember that Criswell hates failure. He has from childhood. "If our foresight were as accurate as our hindsight we would all be better off" is an axiom he often quotes. Criswell is incredibly disciplined. He is a perfectionist. He always carries exactly $37.00 in cash—a $20 bill, a ten, a five, and two ones—"a bill for any expenditure."

GREAT VISION

Criswell believes that each church, in time, is a reflection of its pastor. "After five years a church becomes like its pastor. . . . The congregation reflects his persuasions and convictions."[18] Therefore, Criswell is strong on leadership. He is a "mover and shaker" and expects his associates to be as well. This attitude has caused the church to grow and accomplish feats most people would consider impossible. After all, how many local churches own more than $100 million of real estate? This philosophy says "Have great vision! You are only limited by your own limited vision."

POSTERITY

Criswell has brought a spirit of excellence to the church. He wants his influence passed on to future generations. He has started a college, grade school, radio station, and mission churches. He wants his influence to be felt for years to come, not so much for his sake, but for the sake of conservative evangelical theology. Criswell will be remembered in church history for many things, but perhaps nothing will have a more long-lasting effect than his position on conservative theology.

When liberalism abounded, Criswell never moved. Many pastors of the largest churches in America found strength and guidance from Criswell during those times and now emulate him and his theological position. This attitude has given the church and staff a sense of destiny. This philosophy says "Pass your religious beliefs on to the next generation. The history of the Christian church will probably not end with you. Plan for the future of the church as well as for the present."

STERNNESS

To Criswell, sternness produces results. At least it did in his life. Dr. Armstong and Dr. Robertson were stern men. His mother was stern about his education, and he sees where it led him. He earned a Ph.D. degree when many other preachers had never attended seminary. He was told to study, study, study when he was growing up. He did then. He does now.

Fifty-one books, hundreds of articles, thousands of sermons, and millions of dollars later Criswell sees the fruits. Sternness produces results. Therefore, even though he is a gracious man, he can burn holes through you with his eyes. He will praise you publicly, and he will rebuke you publicly. He explodes in anger at times, and you want to "crawl under the floor." But Criswell keeps short accounts. He will forgive. But he expects people to learn from their mistakes and go on with life. Criswell says, "Don't reprimand staff or leaders publicly. Do it privately, and then with love and grace."[19] Criswell does not always follow his own advice.

ENCOURAGEMENT

Visitors to First Baptist Church often leave saying, "Even though it is a large church, it is such a friendly church." That is because Criswell's philosophy is to "rave" over people. At Baylor, Dr. Trantham and President Brooks encouraged Criswell greatly by stating their confidence in him. Criswell learned at a young age what an encouraging word could mean. He encourages people personally and publicly. He makes you feel like you can do just about anything. His encouraging nature has spread throughout the church and has become part of the philosophy used by the staff: encourage (don't manipulate) other people, and they will respond.

ACTIVITY

Criswell's formula for success is simple: activity and involvement result in growth and productivity. The catalyst of Criswell's tenure at First Baptist Church can be clearly seen in one area, namely, building programs. When at Chickasha and Muskogee it was the same. When people are part of a "big cause" they come together, work hard, sometimes fight, but always grow. Buildings are tangible. They can be seen. Growth can be measured. Criswell likes to measure growth, and growth comes by activity and involvement. When nothing is happening, then nothing happens!

EXPANSION

Whenever a big opportunity occurs, Criswell never looks at it as an end in itself. Criswell always sees a big opportunity as a road to a bigger opportunity. In October 1985, the church was beginning its annual stewardship campaign. To some that would appear to be a bad time to have a special offering, but "the first Sunday in October marked forty-one years at First Baptist for Criswell. That day he used the occasion to challenge his congregation to contribute $1,000,000.00. When the offering was tallied, the $1.85 million total was front page news."[20] This philosophy regarding the programming of the church has been used successfully many times in many ways. Turn big opportunities into bigger opportunities. When an opportunity for expansion presents itself, take a leadership role and expand in every area possible.

ONE HUNDRED PERCENT PARTICIPATION

Criswell believes solidly in the educational philosophy that holds "We learn by doing." It matters not that a person does not know how to do a task or job in the church. He can learn. Everybody needs to feel that they are part of the group. People learn by having a job to do. Involvement in learning produces good results. Even when simply making a public announcement you should do something (sing a song or perform a skit). Just talking does not cause anyone to feel involved in the learning process. Criswell's contribution here is to encourage every member of the church to be actively involved in a ministry. In this manner all are present, feel like they are part of the group, and learn while they "are doing."

BEING YOURSELF

The educational staff members are not expected to be "Criswell clones." He wants each person on the staff to "be yourself." His speech teacher taught him years ago, "You are the best *you* anybody can be." He still believes that. The philosophy is to learn what you can from others, understand and find out what needs to be done, then do it. Do it right, but be yourself as you do it. Do not be a cheap imitation of someone else. This frees the church staff to be creative in many endeavors.

SHOWING FEELINGS

The next educational contribution of Criswell is his belief that one way to get people to do what you want them to do is to show your feelings. That is, if it is a good situation, outwardly show your excitement and enthusiasm. If it is a bad situation, outwardly show your disappointment. People respond better if they know exactly where you stand and where they stand. Criswell gets people to feel like they are part of a team, of which he is the coach. He is trying to produce a winning team and wants his people to respond accordingly. He believes that if he shows how he feels, the people respond better.

Criswell has shaped the educational philosophy of the church by paying tribute to other people. Buildings, plazas, chapels, auditoriums, dining rooms, and halls are all named in someone's honor or memory. In this way the current generation is tied with the past and future. People do not feel that they are an "island unto themselves." They are a part of history, and they too will be remembered in the future. Criswell continues to pay tribute to Truett each year on the anniversary of his death by preaching a sermon in his honor. He refers to him as "the great Truett." Criswell often says, "I am so unworthy to be here. I am just a country preacher. I feel the same way I did sixty years ago when I pastored my first church as a youth." Whoever takes Criswell's place will be wise to remember Criswell as well. To honor and remember others is a philosophy that has been built into the mindset of the membership of First Baptist Church.

EMPHASIS ON YOUTH

Criswell believes that one of the keys to church growth is building the youth departments. His thesis is that parents will go to the church their children want to attend. Therefore, children's programs get much attention, for they are a central part of Criswell's philosophy of building the educational program of the church. Closely related to this philosophy is an emphasis on the "Young Married Couples" department. To Criswell, young married families are the future of the church.

PEOPLE CENTERED

As odd as it may sound, Criswell does not believe a church ever has a money problem. To him it is always a "people problem." When people are present, they give and support the work of the church. If people get involved in the life and activities of the church, their money will follow. Therefore, the philosophy of educational programming is not, "How much does it cost?" but rather, "Can we get people to come and be part of the program?"

THE WINNING ATTITUDE

Perhaps the greatest educational philosophy Criswell has built into the church is the concept "You are a winner!" Criswell has a close walk with God and feels a strong sense of the eternal. Criswell believes that he is a winner, as is every person who is a Christian. Patterson succinctly notes, "One staff member made the sage comment that 'if the whole world were one game of musical chairs with all four billion people involved and only one chair, when the music stopped no one would have to guess who would be in the chair: it would be W. A. Criswell.'"[21]

Conclusion

The main factor influencing Criswell has been people. He has always been sensitive to the attitudes and feelings of those close to him. In the *Dallas Morning News*, Criswell was asked, "If I could change one thing about myself it would be . . ." He answered, "To not let things get to me."[22] Criswell seemingly has a love for everybody and does not want to intentionally hurt anyone, even his opponents. His positive outlook on life makes him respected by all.

As Criswell was growing up, he was influenced by his mother, George W. Truett, S. P. Brooks, Dr. Armstrong, Dr. Trantham, Dr. Robertson, and Dr. Davis. By the time Criswell received his doctorate of philosophy it seems he had decided to become an influence himself. Other than the notes on expositional preaching from the library of A. N. Hall, Criswell appears to have been swayed little by outside influences as far as his educational programming and pastoring skills are concerned.

The question is often raised, "Who will take the place of W. A. Criswell when he is gone?" The answer is obvious, "Nobody!" No one could ever take the place of W. A. Criswell. However, just as Criswell never tried to be George W. Truett, the next pastor of First Baptist Church will not seek to be W. A. Criswell. Rather he will seek to be God's man for that hour.

Notes

1. T. Charlton and R. Spain, *Oral Memoirs of W. A. Criswell* (Waco, Tex.: Baylor U., 1973), p. 175.
2. W. A. Criswell, *Criswell's Guidebook for Pastors* (Nashville: Broadman, 1980), p. 46.
3. Charlton and Spain, *Oral Memoirs*, p. 193.
4. Ibid., pp. 190-91.
5. D. Jennings, "High Profile: W. A. Criswell," *Dallas Morning News*, 1 December 1985, p. 4E.
6. Leon McBeth, *The First Baptist Church of Dallas* (Grand Rapids: Zondervan, 1968), p. 286.
7. Charlton and Spain, *Oral Memoirs*, p. 284.
8. Ibid., p. 200.
9. McBeth, *The First Baptist Church of Dallas*, pp. 322-23.
10. Charlton and Spain, *Oral Memoirs*, p. 283.
11. W. A. Criswell, letter to his church staff, 9 April 1984.
12. McBeth, *The First Baptist Church of Dallas*, pp. 333-34.
13. Ibid., p. 326.
14. Charlton and Spain, *Oral Memoirs*, p. 173.

15. Ibid., p. 255.
16. Criswell, *Criswell's Guidebook*, p. 89.
17. W. A. Criswell, "The Fifth Commandment," sermon preached at First Baptist Church, 5 May 1988.
18. Dick Reavis, "The Politics of Armageddon," *Texas Monthly*, (October 1984), p. 242.
19. Criswell, *Criswell's Guidebook*, p. 372.
20. Jennings, "High Profile."
21. Patterson, "The Imponderables of God," p. 243.
22. Jennings "High Profile."

Appendix A

TIME LINE—W. A. CRISWELL
(from *Criswell Theological Review* 1, no. 2, pp. 252-53)

1909 Born December 19, Eldorado, Oklahoma.

1916 Moved to farm between Clayton, New Mexico, and Texline, Texas; began grammar school.

1919 Conversion and baptism; baptized by Pastor L. S. Hill.

1921 Revival at Texline under Charles Whaley during which Criswell made commitment to the ministry.

1925 Moved to Amarillo to attend high school.

1927 Licensed to preach by First Baptist, Amarillo (pastor, Dr. G. L. Yates); graduated from high school; matriculated at Baylor University with major in English; first sermon in public square in Waco, Texas; first formal sermon in Baptist Church at Mount Calm, Texas; first public re sponse and first stipend paid.

1928 Ordination at San Jacinto Baptist Church of Amarillo; first pastorate at Devil's Bend in Marlow, Texas; first revival conducted at Bethel Church in Coryll County, Texas; second pastorate at Pecan Grove Baptist, Pulltight, Texas.

* Patterson's time line shows that Criswell was elected president of the Southern Baptist Convention for the first time in 1969. Criswell was actually elected president for the first time in 1968 in Houston, and re-elected in 1969 in New Orleans. Each term was then served the following year.

1929 Third pastorate at Mound, Texas.

1931 Graduated with B.A. degree from Baylor University, Waco, Texas; matriculated at Southern Baptist Theological Seminary, Louisville, Kentucky; pastor at Mount Washington Baptist Church in Bullit County, Kentucky.

1932 Pastor at Oakland Baptist Church and Woodburn Baptist Church in Warren County, Kentucky.

1934 Received Th.M. degree from Southern Baptist Theological Seminary.

1937 Received Ph.D. degree from Southern Baptist Theological Seminary; pastor at First Baptist Church, Chickasha, Oklahoma.

1939 Birth of Mabel Anne, first and only child.

1941 Pastor at First Baptist Church, Muskogee, Oklahoma.

1944 Pastor at First Baptist Church, Dallas, Texas.

1945 Awarded Doctor of Divinity degree, Baylor University, Waco, Texas; Dr. Rushbrook, president of Baptist World Alliance, visits First Baptist.

1946 Began eighteen-year program of preaching through the entire Bible.

1950 Published first book, *The Gospel According to Moses.*

1953 Billy Graham Cotton Bowl Crusade; Billy Graham joins First Baptist Church of Dallas.

1957 Published *Did Man Just Happen?*

1961 New Year's Eve's famous "All-Night Sermon," "The Scarlet Thread Through the Bible"; begins publication of five volume *Expository Notes on Revelation.*

1965 Completes *Expository Notes on Revelation*; airplane crash in South American jungle.

1966 Published *The Holy Spirit for Today's World.*

1968 Begins publishing series *Expository Sermons on Daniel*; elected president, Southern Baptist Convention (in Houston).*

1969 Published *Why I Preach the Bible Is Literally True*; presides as president over Southern Baptist Convention (New Orleans); re-elected president, Southern Baptist Convention.

1970 Presides as president, Southern Baptist Convention (Denver); begins Criswell Bible Institute (later The Criswell College); published *The Scarlet Thread.*

1972 Completes publishing *Expository Sermons on Daniel*; begins First Baptist Academy.

1973 Awarded Doctor of Sacred Theology degree, Western Conservative Baptist Theological Seminary.

1975 Awarded Doctor of Letters degree, California Baptist College; awarded Doctor of Letters degree, California Graduate School of Theology; famous sermon "Death in Detente."

1976 Begins Radio Station KCBI-FM; President Gerald Ford visits First Baptist Church in Dallas;

1978 21,000th member joins First Baptist Church.

1979 Published *Criswell Study Bible.*

1980 Published *Criswell's Guidebook for Pastors.*

1985 Addresses 25,000 at Southern Baptist Convention Pastor's Conference with famous sermon on theological liberalism; awarded Doctor of Divinity degree, Hannibal-Lagrange College; Criswell College accredited by Southern Association of Colleges and Schools.

Appendix B

Revival for the Soul

The following is excerpted from an article printed in *Texas Monthly* magazine, October 1984, written by Dick J. Reavis. The full article was entitled "The Politics of Armagaddon."

George W. Truett came to the pulpit he would occupy for forty-seven years in 1897. During his tenure at First Baptist Church, Truett became the most respected preacher in the South, and his church became the Southern Baptist Convention's largest. When he died in 1944, no one thought a pastor could be found who would measure up to him—though many Baptists today feel the same way about W. A . Criswell, the man who did follow Truett. In conduct and tone, Truett is still the yardstick by which Southern Baptist preachers measure themselves. But not in doctrine.

For almost four decades J. Frank Norris was Truett's chief rival for the soul of Texas Baptistdom. From 1909 to 1952 Norris was the pastor of the First Baptist Church in Fort Worth. Eventually his pastorate would surpass Truett's to become the biggest in the Baptist world—though to manage it Norris had to take charge of a second church, in far-off Detroit. He and Truett were as different as the rival cities where they preached. Flamboyant where Truett was dignified, doctrinally strict where Truett was relaxed, Norris was the father of modern Baptist fundamentalism. While Truett sermonized about bigotry abroad, Norris rampaged about vice at home, earning the nickname Texas Tornado. The compassionate Christianity preached by Truett did not inhabit Norris' pulpit. During their lifetimes, Truett was more revered than Norris, but in time Norris would prevail.

Their differences originated with their training. Truett, then a pre-law student, was teaching a Baptist Bible class on Sundays in the tiny North Texas town of Whitewright when his fellow church members voted to draft him into the ministry. Norris decided on the ministry while confined to a wheelchair during adolescence; his mother used his paralysis as an opportunity to teach him the Bible. He had the foresight to see that nonseminarians like Truett were a disappearing breed. After graduating from Baylor he went to seminary at Louisville, Kentucky, where he received his doctorate—a year early—and was class valedictorian.

Truett was not learned in Greek or Hebrew, the languages of the Bible, nor did he regard the Good Book as a hermeneutic problem. In Truett's preaching the Bible was the home base but not the sole province of wide-ranging wisdom. His ministry was not marked by concern for doctrinal questions. Instead, he preached on topics like Christian charity, familial duty, and missionary work. His sermons carried titles like "It Pays to Do Right" and "The Cure for a Troubled Heart." In them he quoted ecumenically from other preachers, world leaders, scientists, and philosophers, even from those whose religious leanings were less than faithful. "Infidel," the favorite derogative of W. A. Criswell, does not appear in Truett's texts.

But Norris was obsessed with doctrine. He attacked fellow Baptists whose theology he found wanting—starting with George W. Truett. Every Sunday morning Norris sent Truett a telegram, which First Baptist deacons tried to intercept. The text was essentially the same: "How can a man like you presume to occupy a Baptist pulpit?" Norris accused Baylor professors of teaching evolution and praising books that, he asserted, said Mary was a whore and Jesus an illegitimate child. He denounced the multiracial World Baptist Alliance as being under the influence of modernism, referring to the Southern Baptist Convention as a "machine" and a "dictatorship," and charged that Truett was shielding both groups. In 1924 the Baptist General Convention of Texas, the state arm of the SBC, ousted the Tornado, but Norris continued the attack in debates and rump sessions at SBC meetings, where W. A. Criswell heard him speak. Depicting himself as a modern-day Martin Luther, persecuted for defending the Bible, Norris founded a denomination of his own, the Premillennial, Fundamental, Missionary Fellowship, usually called the Fundamentalist Baptist Church.

The differences between Truett and Norris extended to preaching style. Norris punctuated his sermons by flailing his arms, kicking his feet, even flinging his coat on the floor. Truett's voice did all the acrobatics; he did not move at all. Sunday after Sunday he stood straight-backed behind the pulpit, as motionless as granite but as moving as the wind. His voice could leap from a whisper to a shout in the utterance of a syllable. His rate of speech, normally a conversational 80 words per minute, could accelerate to bursts of 240. When Truett spoke, his listeners heard the voice of ageless bereavement, of solemn but overwhelming sorrow.

The whole range of poetic techniques was Truett's, as if it were second nature. He spoke strings of alliteration—"busy, battered, burdened humanity," he called us—and could slip into similes "as sincere as sunshine." He created rhythmic, repetitive lines so much like those of a later Baptist preacher, Martin Luther King, Jr. "We're bound together in the bundle of life," Truett preached. "We're bound together in the bundle of life. No man can live to himself, no man can die to himself. we're bound together in the bundle of life." Norris' style was more earthy. His shouts were like savage war whoops; he traded gibes with listeners in the pews; he used such props as a barrel of apples, which he tossed, one at a time, into the congregation, and a head-nodding horse that he ushered into church for a baptismal service.

Truett was best known in Dallas for his Christmas messages, published as newspaper advertisements. He usually opened the sermonettes by assessing the condition of humanity in empathetic, nonsectarian terms. His closing prayers had the ecumenical point of view that Norris scorned as modernism: "May our consciences be so acutely quickened that we shall feel the sin and shame of selfish war and private greed and whatever alienates life from life, class from class, and nation from nation." Norris made his name by stalking, cornering and vanquishing commercial vice, more vituperatively and more successfully than any Texas preacher before or since. The seminary he founded (now Arlington Baptist College) stands on a site once occupied by a silk-stocking gambling club that was shut down at the Tornado's insistence.

Empathy was Truett's medium. He had no use for money and often told his friends, who vainly tried to teach him different, that it was useful only to ease the burdens of the poor. Beggars painted red arrows on the curbs, pointing the way to his house. None went away empty-handed. So generous was Truett that the church payroll office, in conspiracy with his wife, didn't put his full salary in his hands. The congregation also initiated a tradition that has devolved upon the more prosperous Criswell: individual members bought clothing and other durables as gifts to the pastor.

Norris had no compassion for those who drew his wrath, and they were many. He preached sermons with titles like "Should a Prominent Fort Worth Banker Buy High-Priced Silk Hose for Another Man's Wife?" And J. Frank did not shrink from naming names. The wealthy and well-placed were his targets, and his tactics (he was one of the first preachers to advertise his sermons, using radio, newspapers, handbills, and sound trucks) drew great throngs of working-class people to his church. In 1926 the Tornado shot a man dead during an argument that, according to his confidant and biographer, followed a radio sermon in which he had identified the man as an adulterer. He was acquitted. He was tried for arson after First Baptist burned to the ground—and acquitted. When the attorney who had prosecuted him died in a collision with a streetcar, Norris took a broken whiskey bottle, filled with what he said was the man's brains, to the pulpit and preached a sermon entitled, "The Wages of Sin Is Death."

Truett's sermons, his bearing, his impeccable decency, earned him a wide following outside his own denomination and his own city. He became president of the Southern Baptist Convention and later of the World Baptist Alliance. He was sought by pulpit committees across the nation and, according to legend, refused an appeal from John D. Rockefeller to pastor the tycoon's home church. A Houston newspaper once editorialized that the only Dallas skyscraper Houston really coveted was George W. Truett. When the beloved pastor died in 1944, his funeral, attended by eight thousand people, was described by the *Dallas Morning News* as the largest in Texas history.

J. Frank Norris was buried in 1952, accompanied by the wails and tears of five thousand mourners. He was outspoken to the end. He did not live to see his theology gain widespread acceptance, but he had scattered seeds that would sprout in time. He had been the first to champion a young missionary named John Birch, who had trained at Norris' Fort Worth seminary. After Birch was murdered by Chinese communists in 1945, Norris named a Sunday School building in his honor. Norris's Detroit Sunday school superintendent had founded a fundamentalist seminary that one day would train Moral Majority leader Jerry Falwell. And he had seen the pulpit occupied for so many years by his archenemy, George W. Truett, pass to W. A. Criswell. . . .

There is one more incident in this article that must be recounted regarding Norris:

Already Criswell was widely known as the fastest-rising star in the Baptist firmament. His biblical sermons and his church-building also drew the notice of a preacher closer to home. One afternoon in 1952, while working in his church-office study, he glanced out the door that led to a waiting room. A familiar figure was seated there, waiting with great patience. Criswell buzzed his secretary.

"Do you see that old man out there?" he asked. "How long has he been waiting?"

"Well, he's been there for quite a while, Dr. Criswell. He looked like a bum to me, and I wasn't sure you'd want to be disturbed," the secretary told him.

"That man is Frank Norris!" the pastor erupted. Criswell went outside, threw his arms around J. Frank, and invited him into the study.

"My Lord! What brings you here?" he asked.

"Why, I just wanted to know how you are doing," the Tornado told him.

"Oh, we're doing great. We've been blessed, and our work is going ahead wonderfully," the younger preacher said.

"Well, God bless you, that's all I wanted to hear,"

Norris stammered as he turned to go. He didn't say another word, and soon his words were no more: days later the Tornado died while attending a youth rally in Florida. His visit—or was it a pilgrimage?—to First Baptist was testimony to how much the church had changed since the days when George Truett had trembled as he read J. Frank's Sunday morning telegrams (p. 242).

Appendix C

First Baptist Church Statistics, 1944-1989

Church Year	*Church Members*	*Sunday School Enrollment*	*Additions by Baptism*	*Total Additions*	*Total Gifts*
1944	7,804	3,940	84	419	256,302
1945	8,253	4,144	221	888	377,151
1946	8,475	4,381	162	819	406,546
1947	8,636	4,346	175	753	454,020
1948	8,724	4,373	133	628	558,838
1949	8,913	4,842	269	874	586,029
1950	9,128	5,182	270	849	562,100
1951	9,383	5,413	271	897	724,435
1952	9,640	5,793	241	892	721,192
1953	10,046	6,082	272	975	1,762,599
1954	10,523	5,915	315	1,116	1,180,455
1955	11,115	6,470	311	1,290	1,342,223
1956	11,481	7,156	435	1,531	1,211,009
1957	10,851	7,320	314	1,170	1,300,364
1958	11,883	7,719	373	1,224	1,202,415
1959	11,492	7,954	328	1,122	1,425,128

DR. C

1960	12,108	7,745	256	1,003	1,488,568
1961	12,477	7,397	397	1,245	1,556,980
1962	12,879	8,046	406	1,325	1,479,950
1963	13,142	8,116	269	1,116	1,459,921
1964	12,291	8,322	301	1,111	1,588,099
1965	13, 538	8,323	277	1,122	1,597,805
1966	13,971	8,327	322	1,238	1,794,892
1967	14,468	8,414	261	1,190	1,926,904
1968	14,825	8,655	310	1,232	2,220,141
1969	15,451	8,981	276	1,281	2,595,800
1970	15,929	9,449	381	1,382	3,464,250
1971	16,609	9,422	434	1,470	3,344,063
1972	17,280	10,251	443	1,542	3,967,956
1973	17,867	10,200	431	1,459	4,565,825
1974	18,506	10,558	537	1,568	5,297,062
1975	18,948	10,759	430	1,442	5,666,391
1976	18,869	10,368	425	1,408	5,897,712
1977	19,471	10,563	405	1,242	6,210,825
1978	20,045	11,717	436	1,354	6,860,591
1979	21,093	10,085	663	1,688	7,200,000
1980	21,793	10,892	630	1,561	7,800,000
1981	22,732	10,687	1,084	1,746	9,600,000
1982	23,331	9,762	1,034	1,649	9,000,000
1983	24,429	11,005	1,182	1,923	9,101,151
1984	25,362	11,640	984	1,763	9,765,652
1985	26,269	11,835	1,135	1,882	12,347,612
1986	26,905	12,018	1,029	1,785	13,444,721
1987	27,655	12,035	919	1,519	14,787,743
1988	28,196	12,051	683	1,277	12,398,391
1989	27,580	11,728	432	880	9,790,958

Appendix D

Graded Sunday School Program

Cradle Roll	A home ministry to First Baptist members who have a new baby until the baby is brought to the Nursery; an outreach ministry to prospective families with a child under two years of age; a home ministry to expectant families
Nursery Division	Children less than three years old
Beginner Division	Four years old to first grade
Primary Division	First grade through third grade
Junior Division	Fourth grade through sixth grade
Youth Division	Seventh grade through eighth grade (junior high)
	Ninth grade through twelfth grade (senior high)
College Division	Students enrolled in college
Singles division	Singles aged 20 and up; divided into smaller groups based on age, some in graduate school
Young Career	Mostly singles aged 20-35; meet in large group
Young Marrieds	Married—aged 20-30
Young Adults	Married—aged 31-40
Median Adults	Married—aged 41-50
Meredian Adults	Married—aged 51-60
Senior Adults	Married/Widowed—over 60

Appendix E

Bible Division

Classes not divided by age; primarily centered on the teacher; no specific curriculum; however, the Bible is always the primary text.

Bible Division I	Mrs. "C's" Bible Class—taught by Mrs. W. A. Criswell
Bible Division II	Fellowship Class—taught by Doug Brady
	Fuller Class—taught by Margaret Fuller
	Medical and Dental Class—taught by Jack Shaw
	Pathfinder Class—taught by Dr. Eugene Merrill
	Precept Class—taught by June Hunt
	Sheafor Class—taught by Dr. Ray Clendenen
Bible Division III	Executive Class—taught by Dr. Paige Patterson
	President's Class—taught by Dr. Charles Lowery
Bible Division IV	Auditorium Class—taught by Zig Ziglar

Appendix F

Annotated Bibliography of the Works of W. A. Criswell*

In addition to these fifty-one volumes, Criswell has produced numerous articles and booklets that have not been included in this bibliography of major published works.

The Gospel According to Moses. Nashville: Broadman, 1950.
Sixteen sermons trace the theme of "grace" through the Pentateuch as Criswell interprets the Old Testament in light of the New. This volume was reprinted by Zondervan in 1960.

Passport to the World. Nashville: Broadman, 1951.
This book was coauthored with Duke K. McCall and takes Criswell and McCall to all of the mission fields where Southern Baptists were working at the time.

These Issues We Must Face. Grand Rapids: Zondervan, 1953.
In this series of fourteen messages Criswell addresses relevant controversial issues, such as modernism, the

* This compilation was done by Lamar E. Cooper, Sr., professor at The Criswell College, and has been adapted and used by permission.

virgin birth, baptism of the Holy Spirit, and the second coming of Christ.

Did Man Just Happen? Grand Rapids: Zondervan, 1957.

These messages on the first chapter of Genesis set forth the case of creationism and expose the weaknesses of the evolutionary world view.

Five Great Questions of the Bible. Grand Rapids: Zondervan, 1958.

This small volume consists of five messages that follow the theme of the title. Criswell addresses these questions: "Am I My Brother's Keeper?"; "If a Man Dies, Shall He Live Again?"; "What Shall I Do Then with Jesus Which Is Called Christ?"; "What Must I Do to Be Saved?"; and "How Shall We Escape, If We Neglect So Great Salvation?"

Five Great Affirmations of the Bible. Grand Rapids: Zondervan, 1959.

This volume was a sequel to *Five Great Questions.* Once again the pastor selects five passages that are tied by the common theme of "affirmations" as the basis for a sermon series. The five affirmations are these: "In the Beginning—God"; "Thou Art the Christ, the Son of the Living God"; "Christ Died for Our Sins"; "He Rose Again the Third Day"; "Behold, He Cometh with Clouds."

Expository Notes on the Gospel of Matthew. Grand Rapids: Zondervan, 1961.

These nine messages trace the successive development of the theme of "Jesus as Messiah" through the gospel of Matthew. The subdivision of each message analyzed the sections of the gospel.

Expository Sermons on Revelation, Volumes 1-5. Grand Rapids: Zondervan, 1962-66.

In addition to providing eighty-two outstanding expository messages on Revelation, these volumes were the first statement in recent time from a premillennial, pretribulation rapture perspective by a Southern Baptist. In 1969 the five volumes were combined in a one-volume edition.

Our Home in Heaven. Grand Rapids: Zondervan, 1964.

This little volume was prepared especially for use by those who have lost loved ones. Included in the first section are Scriptures of comfort, followed by a brief message, and concluding with poems, all of which have a scriptural basis.

The Bible for Today's World. Grand Rapids: Zondervan, 1965.

The importance and value of this book only is eclipsed only by his later magnum opus on the subject, entitled *Why I Preach The Bible Is Literally True. The Bible for Today's World* contains ten messages affirming the Bible as the infallible, inerrant Word of God.

The Holy Spirit for Today's World. Grand Rapids: Zondervan, 1966.

In an era of charismatic confusion regarding the person, nature, and work of the Holy Spirit, this book addresses the basic issues clearly and forthrightly.

In Defense of the Faith. Grand Rapids: Zondervan, 1967.

This work is a series of five sermons addressing issues for consideration by those who are opponents of the Christian faith, such as the atheist, liberal theologian, Communist, materialist, and sinner.

Why I Preach the Bible Is Literally True. Nashville: Broadman, 1969.

No other book has elicited the praise and criticism from advocates and opponents of the doctrine of infallibility and inerrancy of Scripture as this book by Criswell. Its publication was the catalyst for the modern resurgence of conservative doctrine that has held sway in the Southern Baptist Convention in the last decade.

Preaching at the Palace. Grand Rapids: Zondervan, 1969.

For fifty years, two great preachers, George W. Truett and W. A. Criswell, conducted pre-Easter week noon services at the Palace Theatre in downtown Dallas. This commemorative work traces the fifty-year history of the event. It includes two sermons by Truett and ten messages by Criswell preached the week before Easter in 1968 and 1969.

Look Up, Brother! Nashville: Broadman, 1970.

This book commemorates Criswell's term as president of the Southern Baptist Convention. In it, he gives his observations on the issues that were of primary concern to churches of the convention. He signaled the call for a return to expository preaching and conservative teaching based on a commitment to the Bible as the infallible, inerrant Word of God.

Expository Sermons on Daniel, Volumes 1-4. Grand Rapids: Zondervan, 1968-72.

These four volumes were published in a one-volume edition in 1976. Criswell affirms the historicity of Daniel and the authenticity of his book. The four volumes contain forty-seven expository messages that address the controversial issues of Daniel, such as authorship, date, and interpretation. He presents his messages from a premillennial, pretribulation perspective and also relates Daniel to Revelation.

The Scarlet Thread Through the Bible. Nashville: Broadman, 1971.

On New Year's Eve 1969, the pastor preached this message beginning at 7:30 P.M. and continuing until midnight. There are seven parts to the message, which is based on the theme of redemption through the Bible.

Christ and Contemporary Crises. Dallas: Crescendo, 1972.

This volume contains the five pre-Easter messages for the week before Easter 1972. The contemporary themes include "Christ and the State," "Christ and War," "Christ and Modern Science," "Christ and Communism," "Christ and Death."

The Baptism, Filling and Gifts of the Holy Spirit. Grand Rapids: Zondervan, 1973.

Excerpts from the 1966 volume *The Holy Spirit for Today's World* were compiled into sixteen chapters that address the relevant issues in the charismatic movement. The reprint of this work attests its value in addressing the controversy from a solid biblical perspective.

Expository Sermons on Galatians. Grand Rapids: Zondervan, 1973.

The pastor shares twenty-two expository messages on Galatians. The volume was dedicated to the faculty and student body of the newly established Criswell Bible Institute.

Ephesians: An Exposition. Grand Rapids: Zondervan, 1974.

Here are thirty-six expository messages from Ephesians. The sermons are practical in application and exegetically enlightening for students of the Word.

Expository Sermons on the Epistle of James. Grand Rapids: Zondervan, 1975.

Seventeen expository messages present selected passages from James.

Christ the Savior of the World. Dallas: Crescendo, 1975.

This is another volume of pre-Easter messages from 1974; Christ is the grand theme of the five messages: "Christ the Power of God"; "Christ the Gift of God"; "Christ the Word of God"; "Christ the Way of God"; and "Christ the Man of God."

What to Do Until Jesus Comes Back. Nashville: Broadman, 1975.

The thirteen messages are presented in three parts. Part One presents the *hope* of the second coming, Part Two deals with our *earthly assignment* until His return, and Part Three addresses the matter of *endurance* until Jesus returns.

Welcome Back Jesus! Nashville: Broadman, 1976.

This is an additional thirteen messages on the second coming of Jesus, which came as a sequel to *What to Do Until Jesus Comes Back.*

The Compassionate Christ. Dallas: Crescendo, 1976.

These pre-Easter messages from 1975 present the compassion, love, spirit, tears, and blood of Christ.

Expository Sermons on the Epistles of Peter. Grand Rapids: Zondervan, 1976.

Here are twenty-seven expository messages that present the various themes addressed in the books of First and Second Peter.

Isaiah: An Exposition. Grand Rapids: Zondervan, 1977.

These forty-six messages from Isaiah trace the flow of the gospel through the work of the great prophet. Criswell treats Isaiah in a manner consistent with his stance on the Bible. He considers the whole book to be authentic and handles it with reverence. He affirms the virgin birth in Isaiah 7:14, the suffering Savior in Isaiah 53, and the millennial kingdom in Isaiah 65.

The Christ of the Cross. Dallas: Crescendo, 1977.
This volume is five pre-Easter messages from 1976 focusing on Christ as He faced Calvary.

What a Savior. Nashville: Broadman, 1978.**
The chapters in this work are devoted to the atoning work of the blood of Christ. Each chapter was originally a sermon delivered to the congregation of the First Baptist Church, Dallas.

With a Bible in My Hand. Nashville: Broadman, 1978.
This volume commemorated the fiftieth year of the pastor's preaching ministry. Containing his sixteen favorite messages, the volume appeared as the pastor prepared to observe his thirty-fifth year as undershepherd of the First Baptist Church of Dallas.

Acts: An Exposition, Volumes I-III. Grand Rapids: Zondervan, 1978-80.
A one-volume edition of these messages from Acts was published in 1983. Volume I contains thirty-six messages covering Acts 1-8. The second volume contains forty-four messages from Acts 9-18. The last volume contains forty-three messages from Acts 19-28.

The Criswell Study Bible. Nashville: Thomas Nelson, 1979.
The comprehensive notes make this one of the finest study Bibles available. In addition to comments on all major doctrinal passages, the volume deals with problem passages and difficult verses. Charts clarify the feasts and offerings of Israel, the seven churches of Revelation, etc. Each book of the Bible is introduced with a discussion of date, authorship, theme, and special features. Additional helps are in the back, including a concordance and maps.

The Doctrine of the Church. Nashville: Broadman, 1980.
This book was prepared as the doctrinal Bible study for

** This book was inadvertently omitted from the original list compiled by Dr. Cooper. It was added for clarification and completion.

Southern Baptist churches in 1980. Criswell discusses the origin, nature, mission, organization, ordinances, and future of the church.

Criswell's Guidebook for Pastors. Nashville: Broadman, 1980.

The pastor devotes twenty-one chapters to the wisdom of his fifty-six years as a pastor. He gives practical advice in such areas as pulpit presence, sermon preparation, church finance, church administration, and especially helpful advice on the pastor's personal life.

Abiding Hope. Grand Rapids: Zondervan, 1981.

This daily devotional guide is designed for a year's daily use. This book is a series of vignettes for the days of the year taken from the previous writings of Criswell. An index in the back acknowledges the sources of the devotions.

Great Doctrines of the Bible, Volumes I-VI. Grand Rapids: Zondervan, 1982-86.

To date, six volumes have been released in this latest series of messages to be placed in print. They concern the areas of bibliography, theology, Christology, ecclesiology, pneumatology, soteriology, the Christian life, and stewardship. Criswell preached these messages over a three-year period with his goal being to address all the major doctrinal areas of theology. Nine volumes have been planned for the series, with volume seven addressing prayer and angelology and the last two volumes devoted to eschatology.

Appendix G

The Southern Baptist Holy War, Joe Edward Barnhart (Austin, Tex.: Texas Monthly 1986). 273 pp. reviewed by W. A. Criswell, *Criswell Theological Review* (1988): 453-56.

Joe Edward Barnhart, distinguished professor at North Texas State University, is a philosopher who writes with the communicative skills of a novelist. The combination is a salubrious one. Whether or not one agrees with his conclusions, one will find this book to be enjoyable, infuriating, enlightening, confusing, endearing, and irritating—but never dull. The author is no stranger to the Southern Baptist Zion. Dr. Barnhart studied at Southern Baptist Theological Seminary in Louisville, Kentucky. Formerly a confessing Christian and Baptist, Dr. Barnhart has obviously spent much time in pursuit of the "facts" in the controversy, which has spanned the last nine years in Southern Baptist life.

Barnhart's casual style, however, does not succeed in distguishing a pervasive carelessness in research, which is particularly unworthy of a son of Socrates. Undocumented avowals and lengthy opinions void of substantive support abound. Even a lofty academe may be justified in the writing of prose for a popular market, choosing not to follow the canons of accuracy and the demand of documentation normally anticipated in a technical work. But a plethora of factual errors undermines the credibility of any author, philosophers included.

For example, Lee Roberson will probably be surprised to learn that he was never a Southern Baptist (p. 148). Charles Stanley and his children may be amused to discover that the popular pastor urged his children not to attend Southern Baptist schools (p. 4). H. L. Hunt became a Christian and joined the First Baptist Church of Dallas rather late in life and was not a "member for many years" (p. 217). Barnhart totally misleads the reader regarding J. L. Dagg, calling him a "racial bigot," and alleging that he spent much of his life attempting to justify slavery (p. 130). Actually, Dagg wrote five excellent books. Only in his *Moral Science* did he make an abortive attempt to justify slavery, and this attempt occupied a small section of the monograph. Neither did such discussions occupy much of the time of this noble pastor and former president of Mercer University. There are examples of the egregious errors of fact which mar the effort.

Worse still are the apparent misrepresentations of the views and statements of others. My assistant, Dr. Paige Patterson, is represented as not desiring to have his money pay the salary of a professor who presents a view other than his own (p. 98). Aside from the fact that Patterson is misrepresented, Barnhart fails to explain how it is that views differing markedly from Patterson's own are presented and sometimes even advocated by professors in the Criswell College, over which Patterson presides as President.

My own position is misrepresented by Professor Barnhart when he alleges that "pressed to the wall, Criswell and his brothers in inerrancy can produce no good reason to deny women ordination except that God does not want them ordained" (p. 152). My theology does, in fact, maintain that an explicit word from God in the Bible is adequate for faith and practice. However, absence of any evidence cited to indicate that this is my view of the ordination of women serves as a stern reminder to the reader that Barnhart has an inappropriate tendency to create positions for others as he goes along, charmed as he apparently is by the illusionary character of his own visions of how things are.

A veneer of scholarship dignifies the treatise with documentation in nine pages of endnotes and an index. The latter is excellent, but the former betrays inadequate research. Assertions of what others believe are often stated with the abandon of a television news commentator. No evidence is cited. Not infrequently some "proponent" is quoted but never identified. For example, "Tillich is a bridge, all right. . . . He's a bridge that leads the innocent out of the clear air of orthodoxy and into the rain of heresy" (p. 133). We must ask, who said this? The answer may be that this book is not intended to be serious history. It is a *Texas Monthly* popular mythology. But the preface of *The Southern Baptist Holy War* seems to suggest a serious attempt to be objective and accurate. In discussing a confrontation involving the lives of nearly fifteen million people, Barnhart should have honored the tested methods of research and reporting that are insisted upon by scholars in the academy.

Finally, the approach which Barnhart makes is somewhat enigmatic. Some chapters seem to treat current circumstances or provide appropriate foundation. Others seem at best tenuously related to the controversy he seeks to chronicle. For example, in a long chapter entitled "Jesus Loves Everybody, Especially Winners," Barnhart discusses subjects such as Baptists and faith-healers. Incorporated into these narratives are such figures as Oral Roberts, Jimmy Swaggart, and the neo-Pentecostals. Yet never is there indication of exactly how this information assists the reader in understanding the story of the present Southern Baptist controversy. Inordinate space is allotted to some people who are no longer major players. T. C. Smith, once dismissed from the faculty of Southern Seminary, is a case in point. From reading this book one would naturally assume that Dr. Smith has been the major voice of the liberals when, in fact, he has made little impact even during the days of conflict thirty years ago at Southern Seminary.

On the other side, the scintillating style of the book is not its only virtue. Conservative Southern Baptists will welcome the book for several reasons. First, Dr. Barnhart provides "exhibit A" for legitimacy of their concerns. Presumably, Barnhart believed in God when he entered Southern Seminary. In an enlightening section of chapter three entitled "Thunderstruck at the Seminary," the author describes the shaking of the faith of students arriving for studies in many seminaries. Though he does not say as much, the description has an autobiographical ring. Is it possible that what is here described is the seminary pilgrimage of Joe Edward Barnhart from belief in God to his present agnosticism? In the midst of this, a stunning admission will arrest the reader. "Critics of the seminaries are doubtless correct to charge that much of the biblical criticism taught in the seminary classrooms exacts a heavy toll from these Baptist men and women" (p. 42). Such honesty is refreshing to those of us who have endured a duplicitous Baptist form of "Jesuitical casuitry" on the part of liberals among Southern Baptists.

Furthermore, Dr. Barnhart knows what the real questions are. "Is there a Supreme Intelligence who has designed this vast and complex universe? And if there is, has this Being communicated in some way with mortal humans who occupy a tiny pocket of the universe?" (p. 40). Or again, "If Christians are left to sift through the Bible to separate the credible from the incredible, will the Bible no longer be the Christian's final court of appeal? Will there be any final court of appeal?" (p. 35).

In short, misrepresentations notwithstanding, Barnhart understands the seminal questions and the matrix of conservative Southern Baptist thinking far better than most of the moderate or liberal leaders and professors in the denomination. For these reasons every interested Southern Baptist and every conservative evangelical should read this book.

Through the occasionally absurd analogies, non-sequiturs, misrepresentations, and thinly disguised polemics against the faith of conservative evangelicals, one of the author's misunderstandings emerges like Poseidon from the sea. Dr. Barnhart appears to think that good education presents and criticizes all options while advocating none. Yet I doubt that he would wish to accredit a medical school which had such a pedagogical approach. Further, he seems to be oblivious to the fact that like all human authors and instructors, he, too, has an axe to grind—and he does so very fine!

Should you read this book? Of course. And read about Uncle Remus and Tar Baby, too! Enjoy both! Get all you can from both! Don't take either too seriously!

Appendix H

Joining the Church

W. A. Criswell, Pastor, First Baptist Church.

This booklet is given to each person who joins the church.
It was written especially for children.

When I was a little boy and gave my heart to the Lord, I was immediately baptized; but no one said anything to me about the meaning of the holy ordinance. It was only in after years that I learned its true and beautiful significance. I made a resolution when I began my pastoral ministry that every child who came forward to be baptized would be faithfully taught the scriptural meaning of the ordinance. This little book is the fruit of that resolution. May it prove a blessing to every child and to everyone who studies it. (W. A. Criswell)

Chapter 1
What It Means to Be Saved

Without Christ as my Savior I am a condemned sinner (John 3:18). I am utterly lost (John 3:36). As a condemned sinner I am spiritually dead (Ephesians 2:1). I have no hope and I am without God in the world (Ephesians 2:12).

But when Christ comes into my heart, He forgives my sin (Acts 10:43), He writes my name in the Book of Life (Revelation 21:27), He saves my soul (Luke 19:10). Believing in Christ as my Savior, I am a new creation (II Corinthians 5:17). I am a child of God (John 1:12).

For Christ to be a Savior to me I must realize that I am a lost sinner and that He came into the world to save me (Isaiah 53:6; I Timothy 1:15; Matthew 1:21). I am saved forever by repenting of my sins (Luke 13:3) and believing in Jesus as my Savior (John 3:14-16; John 5:24; Acts 20:21; II Timothy 1:12).

When I repent of my sins and ask Jesus to save me, I am immediately and publicly to confess Him as my Savior and Lord (Matthew 10:32, 33; Romans 10:9, 10).

Questions and Answers

Question: From what does Jesus save?

Answer: From our sins (Mark 2:1-11; Matthew 26:28; I John 1:7).

Question: What is sin?

Answer: Sin is disobedience to God, breaking the law of God (I John 3:4).

Question: Who has sinned?

Answer: All of us have sinned. I have sinned. We all have sinned (Romans 3:10, 23).

Question: What is the penalty for my sin?

Answer: Death (Ezekiel 18:4; Romans 6:23):

(1) Physical Death: The soul separated from the body.

(2) Spiritual Death: The second death. The soul is separated from God forever.

Question: How can I be saved from this death?

Answer: I can be saved from eternal death by trusting Jesus as my Savior. I am sorry for my sin and turn from it (this is repentance) and look to Jesus to forgive me (this is saving faith) (Acts 16:30, 31).

Question: Do I work for this great salvation?

Answer: I do not work for my salvation. It is a free gift of God. It is wholly of grace. I just receive it; I just take it; I just accept it. My salvation is something God gives me through faith in Jesus Christ (Romans 4:5; Ephesians 2:8, 9).

Question: Why should I seek to do good works?

Answer: Because Jesus has saved me and I seek to honor Him in my life (Ephesians 2:10; James 2:26; John 15:14). If I am truly saved, I will obey my Lord. Good works are the result of my salvation, not the means by which I obtain it. Only after the tree is made good can it bring forth good fruit (Matthew 12:33).

Question: What are the steps of salvation as we turn in saving faith to Jesus?

Answer: The steps of salvation are:

(1) Repentance: Being sorry for my sin and turning from my sin to Jesus.
(2) Faith: Accepting Jesus as my Savior.
(3) Confession: Publicly declaring my faith in Jesus.

Chapter 2
What It Means to Be Baptized

The "doctrines" of a church are its beliefs and teachings. The "ordinances" of a church are its observances, called "ordinances" because Christ commanded or "ordered" them. In a New Testament church there are two "ordinances." These two ordinances are baptism and the Lord's Supper.

Baptism is a burial and a resurrection. We are

buried with Christ in the likeness of His death and we are raised with Christ in the likeness of His resurrection (Romans 6:2, 3; Colossians 2:12, Galatians 3:27). It shows forth three things:

1. It portrays or pictures the death, burial and resurrection of Jesus.
2. It portrays or pictures our death to sin and our resurrection to a new life in Christ.
3. It proclaims our faith. Our faith is that if we die and are buried, we shall be raised from the dead by the power of the Lord.

Baptism is the first of the two church ordinances. It is the doorway into the church. We are all baptized by the Holy Spirit into the body of Christ. The body of Christ is His church. Water baptism portrays that work of the Spirit that adds us to the body of Christ (I Corinthians 12:13).

Questions and Answers

Question: Who baptized Jesus?
Answer: John the Baptist (Matthew 3:1).
Question: Where was Jesus baptized?
Answer: In the Jordan River (Matthew 3:13). He had to have "much water" (John 3:23).
Question: Why was Jesus baptized?
Answer: To fulfill all righteousness (Matthew 3:15).
Question: What is baptism?
Answer: It is a burial and a resurrection (Colossians 2:12).
Question: What is the meaning of baptism?
Answer: It pictures three things (Romans 6:23; Galatians 3:27):

1. It pictures the death, burial and resurrection of Jesus.
2. It pictures our death to sin and our resurrection to a new life in Christ.

3. It pictures our faith that if we die and are buried we shall also be raised from the dead.

Question: Does Jesus command us to be baptized?

Answer: Yes. According to His Great Commission in Matthew 28:18-20, all are to be baptized who accept Jesus as their Savior.

Question: In what name are we commanded to be baptized?

Answer: In the name of the Father and the Son and of the Holy Spirit (Matthew 28:19).

Question: In Acts 8:26-39, what was the first thing the eunuch wanted to do after he heard the gospel of Jesus?

Answer: He wanted to be baptized (Acts 8:36).

Question: What was the one requirement he had to meet before he could be baptized?

Answer: To believe in Jesus with all his heart (Acts 8:37).

Question: How was the eunuch baptized?

Answer: He was lowered beneath the baptismal waters (buried with Christ) and he was raised out of the baptismal waters (resurrected with Christ) (Acts 8:38, 39).

Question: According to Acts 2:41; 10:44-48, who should be baptized?

Answer: Those who have repented of their sins and have accepted Jesus as their Savior.

Question: Are we lost if we are not baptized?

Answer: The Bible says we are lost if we do not repent (Luke 13:3). The Bible says we are lost if we fail to believe on Jesus (John 3:18). Nowhere does the Bible say we are lost if we are not baptized.

Question: Why then should we be baptized?

Answer: Because of our love for the Savior. Jesus Himself set the example and Jesus Himself commanded us to be baptized. Baptism is an act of obedience on the part of the one who believes in Jesus.

Question: How is baptism rightly administered?

Answer: The believer is immersed in water, in the name of the Father, and of the Son and of the Holy Spirit. This is according to the institution of Christ and the practice of the Lord's Apostles.

Chapter 3
What It Means to Take the Lord's Supper

The second (and recurring) church ordinance is the Lord's Supper. It was instituted by our Savior the night in which He was betrayed and delivered to die for our sins on the cross (Matthew 26:20-30). We are not saved by partaking of the Supper. It is a memorial of the death of Christ, that we may ever remember His sacrifice for us (I Corinthians 10:16).

Who may take the Lord's Supper? Those who have trusted Jesus as their Savior and who have been baptized in obedience to His command. In the Great Commission recorded in Matthew 28:19, 20, three things are very plain: first, we are to make disciples (the literal translation) of all nations; second, we are to baptize these converts in the name of the Father and of the Son and of the Holy Spirit; third, we are to teach converts to observe the things Jesus has commanded us, one of those things commanded being the observance of the Lord's Supper. The order Jesus gave is very plain. It is one, two, three. One, we must trust Jesus, become a disciple of Jesus. Two, we are to be baptized, "buried with the Lord, raised with the Lord." Three, we are to observe the things Christ has given us to keep, one of which is the Lord's Supper.

This order of one, two, three is as much inspired as

the content of the Great Commission. Before I have the privilege of taking the Lord's Supper I must (first) be converted, I must (second) be baptized, then I am ready (third) to sit at the Lord's table.

Questions and Answers

Read I Corinthians 11:23-29

Question: What are the two elements of the Lord's Supper?

Answer: Bread and "the fruit of the vine" (Matthew 26:29), the red juice of crushed grapes held in a cup.

Question: What do these two elements symbolize?

Answer: The bread represents the body of Christ and the cup represents the blood of Christ.

Question: Why are these two elements not the actual body and blood of Jesus?

Answer: Because when Jesus instituted the Lord's Supper and said these words, His body was standing before the disciples and His blood was still coursing through His veins. The bread and the cup "show forth the Lord's death." The very words "in remembrance of me" suggest their symbolic nature. Jesus said He was "the door" (John 10:9), "the vine" (John 15:1), "the Good Shepherd" (John 10:11), and we understand perfectly what He meant. We understand also the symbolic meaning of His words regarding the bread and the cup.

Question: How often should we observe memorial of the Lord's Supper?

Answer: Jesus left that to us. He said, "as often as ye eat this bread and drink this cup . . ." We could observe the Lord's Supper every day, every week, every month, every quarter.

Question: How should we take the Lord's Supper?
Answer: We should take the Lord's Supper in deepest humility and reverence.

The adverb "unworthily" (notice it is not an adjective) in I Corinthians 11:27-29 refers to our manner of observing the ordinance, not our own worth. Because we are sinners and the sacrifice of Christ has made atonement for our sins, we observe the Lord's Supper in overflowing love and gratitude.

Question: What is meant by the words in I Corinthians 11:26, "till he come"?
Answer: The words "till he come" plainly teach us that our Lord Jesus will come a second time, which is the joy and hope of all those who truly believe in Jesus (Acts 1:11; I Thessalonians 4:16).

Chapter 4
What It Means to Be a Good Church Member

A church is not the building in which the people meet. A church is a congregation of baptized believers voluntarily associated together for the purpose of proclaiming the gospel, observing the ordinances, and fellowshipping in the love and grace of the Lord Jesus. Jesus founded the church (Matthew 16:18) and so loved it that He gave Himself for it (Acts 20:28, Ephesians 5:25).

Questions and Answers

Question: As a church member should I attend the services of the church?
Answer: According to Hebrews 10:25, "not forsaking

the assembling of ourselves together," I must faithfully attend the services of the church.

Question: As a church member should I witness for Jesus?

Answer: According to Luke 24:45-48, Acts 1:8, we are to witness to the saving grace of Jesus to everyone everywhere.

Question: As a church member should I read my Bible and pray every day?

Answer: According to John 5:39, Acts 17:11, I Timothy 4:13-16, Revelation 1:3, I am faithfully to read my Bible, and according to Luke 18:1, I Thessalonians 5:17, I am to pray always.

Question: Does God have a plan for me to support the church?

Answer: According to I Corinthians 16:1, 2, I am every first day of the week (Sunday) to give to God a proportionate part of my income. The people of God under the law gave at least a tenth (Leviticus 27:30-33). Those who love Jesus will give even more. It is a holy privilege to give (II Corinthians 8:9; II Corinthians 9:6, 7).

Benediction

"Now unto Him that is able to keep you from falling, and to present you faultless before the presence of His glory with exceeding joy, to the only wise God our Savior, be glory and majesty, dominion and power, both now and forever. Amen" (Jude 24, 25).

Appendix I

MISSIONS OF THE FIRST BAPTIST CHURCH, DALLAS

Arab Chapel (Arab)	4th Floor, Criswell Bldg., Dallas
Calvary Chapel (Spanish)	5227 Nomas, Dallas
Cambodian	Virginia & Grigsby, Dallas
El Buen Pastor (Spanish)	1118 N. Carroll, Dallas
Good Shepherd (Tri-ethnic)	842 Hillburn Dr., Dallas
Happy Hill Farm	Star Rt: Hwy 144 (Glen Rose)
Inner City Chapel (Street People)	2515 Ross Avenue, Dallas
Laotian Chapel	3125 Peoria, Dallas
Leland Street Chapel (Black)	4609 Leland, Dallas
Loving Missionary (Black)	4002 S. Denley Drive, Dallas
Meadow Gardens (Tri-ethnic)	2902 McGowan, Dallas
Outreach Baptist Chapel	1780 E. Northwest Hwy, Garland
Orchard Road Lewisville	1244 Kingston, Lewisville
Silent Friends (Deaf)	Ralph Baker Hall, FBC
Skyline	3011 Cypress Drive, Dallas
Truett Chapel (Tri-ethnic)	3125 Peoria, Dallas
Mt. Zion Baptist #3 (Black)	515 Long Branch, Dallas
New Mt. Gilead (Black)	1012 Bayonne, Dallas
Brazilian Chapel (Portuguese)	3d Floor, Criswell Bldg., Dallas
Juvenile Ministry	
Youth Village	Hutchins
Harry Hines Detention Ctr.	Harry Hines, Dallas
Dallas House	Military & Buckner, Dallas
Gainesville TDC	Gainesville

Rehab Center	811 S. Akard, Dallas
Prison	State prisons visited by David Umfreville on weekends
Jail	500 Commerce, Dallas Lew Sterrett Center on Oaklawn
*Chinese Chapel	4th floor Criswell Bldg., Dallas
*Japanese Chapel	4th floor Criswell Bldg., Dallas

*These two chapels are more autonomous and do not work directly under the office of Outreach Ministries except in benevolence matters. But Dr. Criswell does refer to them when counting the number of our chapels.

Appendix J

God's Servant,
The Forty Years That Began with Prayer

The following information was transcribed from the slide/tape production that was presented in honor of W. A Criswell's fortieth anniversary as pastor of the First Baptist Church, Dallas. The events of that day were videotaped and are available through the media Ministry of First Baptist Church, Dallas, Texas.

It is morning. The air has that special crystal clarity one feels on the Lord's day. The streets are still. The gray fears of night have fled. The sun grows warm. Soon there will be music from the church . . . over there . . . tough old temple standing among fragile towers. For forty years now, on mornings such as this, we have come to hear the Word, voice of the warm hymn, message from the heart of God to the hearts of men. What would He have us know this day of love and joy, duty, and redemption? For forty years now, we have come to the old stone church to drink at the fountain of the Lord; and for forty years now, it has been this man who has held the cup. (Criswell preaching in the background.)

> "that we build a fence around the cemetery, and that same guy got up. He said, 'I'm agin' it. I'm agin' it.' He said, 'Do you know anybody in that cemetery that can get out?'"
>
> "If there is a preacher who departs from the faith, God sees to it that there is another preacher raised up."
>
> "It is the man. It is the man Christ Jesus. It is He that saves us and it is He that keeps us saved."

Preacher, pastor, shepherd, God's servant. . . . For forty years now, he has nourished our faith, lifted our hearts when they were heavy, touched our children with the song of his spirit. He has fought our most difficult battles and has built our church where it is impossible for a church to be. He has reached out for those among us who are hungry or lost or afraid. He has carved a clean and clear direction for our lives in an age of cruel and confusing ambiguity. We know him as preacher, pastor, shepherd.

But then, sometimes we wonder. Do we really know him at all . . . the man behind the message? Is it even possible that we can know the private person within the public pulpiteer? Isn't he a man, flesh and blood as we are, subject to the same pain and pleasure, which chase each other through our lives? Doesn't the shepherd sometimes fear the wolf, dread the coming of the night? Who is this man that came among us that day so long ago? Remember? He seemed so young. The hands that held the Bible shook. He said there were dozens more qualified than he; but here he was—the unknown man from Muskogee, rock-jawed, eyes on fire—yet warm somehow, even vulnerable—if a tree of a man can be vulnerable. Was he afraid, following the footsteps of the most beloved minister in Christendom, in this world's greatest Baptist church? His text that day was this: "For there stood beside me an angel of God saying, 'Fear not.'" And when his sermon was done, he dropped to his knees before us all and, in this position of humility before God and man, prayed for guidance.

But what do we know of this complex man after all these years we've shared? We know he seems to be a tapestry of contradictions. In the pulpit, he is lightning and thunder; yet out of the pulpit, he is uncommonly shy, beautifully gentle. He has a brilliant mind, is a sophisticated scholar; yet he never allows his scholarship to intrude on the simple truth of his message. He preaches the gospel unadorned. He has enormous dignity, yet will be a clown for a child. He is always surrounded by people but is somehow uniquely, always alone. He is a friend to all, yet allows himself no close friends. He is a rock, yet he weeps before us all. He is elegant and cultured, yet crumbles cornbread in his milk. He works out at the YMCA every day; yet when invited to play golf, he prays for rain. He is courted by many, yet is his own man and does not belong to anyone but God. We know all this, but then, do we really know him at all?

We are, without exception, children of the earth; the land, a crucible of our philosophy. Far out in West Texas there is a place empty as a vagabond's pocket, wide as the horizons of the mind. The boy would have felt the power of this place, its sense of absolutes, its overpowering heat in the summer, the howling blizzards in winter. The sun that falls on the town of Texline casts hard shadows. One rarely finds shades of gray. It was the kind of lonesome land the prophets wandered in another time—both beautiful and incredibly hard.

On a small dirt farm near Texline, the boy sat down one day to read the Bible through, from Genesis to Revelation. He also filled the boredom of long summer days by reading the books of Western tales, the gospel according to Zane Grey, good and evil locked in combat, always won by good. In the Bible, there were bewildering secrets to be unlocked, a code to live by. The West of Zane Grey had its own code.

Once there was a revival meeting in Texline. The people gathered to warm themselves on the fire of their faith. The boy watched and felt the fire and learned the power of the Word to change the hearts of men and women. He knew then what God wanted with his life. He would speak a mosaic of words woven with the power of the Word.

"And Samuel grew, and the Lord was with him and did let none of his words fall to the ground." Now the boy, as a man, is pastor of the largest Baptist church in the world, a preacher of unparalleled power, a denominational leader of unquestioned influence, a shepherd to a flock of twenty-four thousand souls, responsible for a church spreading over six city blocks, filled with the music of twenty choirs, where seven thousand people will attend Sunday school each Sunday, and there will be one thousand baptisms each year. It is a staggering load he carries, yet he shoulders it gladly, with dignity and grace. The day is short, the task so very hard; and he is but a man, flesh and blood as we are. For forty years his sermons have been filled with light; but he is only a man; and in the far corners of the corridors of his mind, there must have sometimes been the darkness of doubt.

The young man in college was pulled two ways. On the one hand, his intellectual curiosity led him inward. He devoured the great philosophies of the ages from St. Augustine to Immanuel Kant."What is the nature of nature? of man? of God? How could it be that so many gifted thinkers have turned away from Christ? Is it possible I've been blinded by the light?" On the other hand, God led him out of the privacy of himself. For the first time the young man saw the world of unfathomable pain and hunger. He preached in jails, the street, the poor house. Here was reality. Here was human need. What does it matter how many angels can fit on the head of a pin when my brother is bleeding and lost? There was no time for doubt—too much to be done. In later years, as a man, he would say this about doubt: "It is a question with which I still wrestle. 'Where is God?' I see the indescribable horror and suffering of war. How does God bear to look upon it? There are inscrutable mysteries into which I cannot enter," the pastor said, "but I am confident of the infinite mercy and goodness of God, and there I stand. . . . I take it by faith." Now he carries his faith out into the city and into the world. His Bible and his bread, his compassion and his Savior, weapons against the problem of evil and the problem of sin and the problem of human need.

Consider God's servant—the preacher, the pastor, the shepherd. For forty years he has preached from that pulpit a timeless truth, which can, and will, never change. God's truth is unalterable—Jesus Christ, the same yesterday, today and forever. It would seem then, that the preacher of that truth would possess a view of the world which would also be unchanged through the years; but on matters of conscience, few men have made the journey the pastor has made; and in this fact resides his greatest humanity.

Years ago his love for his country and his fear of freedom's loss demanded that he step from behind the pulpit and do battle in the secular arena. He fought radicals, atheists, self-serving politicians, runaway liberalism, cowards of all kinds, trendy social patterns, and anyone who would erode the freedoms of action and conscience he so deeply cherished. Then in time, he began to feel his heart changing on one of the more critical issues of his time. No longer did he believe there could be a separation of the races in the Body of Christ. He insisted that the First Baptist Church be a Philadelphian church of the open door. The mind of God is eternal. The heart of man can change.

Another glorious Sunday has said its final "Amen"; and though the old stone church is silent, the memory of hymns sung sweetly hangs in the air. On Swiss Avenue, the preacher, the pastor, the shepherd returns once more to his endless search for answers to inscrutable mysteries; and we wonder, "Who is this man?" We must know. Isn't it necessary that we know so we can express the love we feel, so we can tell him how much he means to our lives? Here is an irony. The fact that he is a giant, that he has accomplished heroic deeds, that he has lived so very close to God sometimes seems to create a distance between us—not of his choosing, nor of ours; but when we reach across that tender distance, now, on this fortieth year he has touched our lives, we build a bridge past pastor, past preacher, past shepherd to the very heart of the man and find there the warmth, the love, and the kinship of a sweet friend and fellow pilgrim: and to him we say, "You are loved. We proudly salute you, W. A. Criswell, our beloved pastor and truly, truly God's Beloved Servant."

Appendix K

SELF-PORTRAIT: HIGH PROFILE. *Dallas Morning News*, 1 DECEMBER 1985

Wallie Amos Criswell

Birthdate and place: Dec. 19, 1909 in Eldorado, Okala.

Occupation: Pastor.

If I've learned one thing in my life, it's: Don't be surprised at anything people do, say or become.

My friends like me because: I am down to earth.

If I could change one thing about myself it would be: To not let things get to me.

My mother's best advice was: Go to school and get a good education.

When I'm nervous: My heart beats faster and my mouth gets dry.

My teen-age idol was: George W. Truett.

The person who had the most impact on my life was: My mother.

Favorite comic strip: Mr. Tweedy, Dennis the Menace, *Peanuts*, *BC* and *Nancy*.

Favorite comedian: Bill Cosby.

Favorite all-time movie: War and Peace.

Favorite all-time television show: I Love Lucy.

Favorite magazine: Christianity Today and Reader's Digest.

Favorite president: Abraham Lincoln.

Behind my back they say: He's a funny-damn-mentalist.

Most valued material possession: Our antique collection.

My best asset is: I am a friendly person.

My worst habit is: I like to eat.

References

Bryson, H. *The Expository Preaching of W. A. Criswell in His Sermons on Revelation.* Doctoral diss., New Orleans Baptist Seminary, 1967.

Charlton, T., and R. Spain. *Oral Memoirs of W. A. Criswell.* Waco, Tex.: Baylor University, 1973.

Criswell, W. A. *The John the Baptist Movement in Its Relation to the Christian Movement.* Doctoral diss., Southern Baptist Theological Seminary, Louisville, 1937.

———. *The Reminder.* A publication of First Baptist Church of Dallas (15 October 1944; 19 November 1944; 3 March 1946; 14 July 1946; 12 September 1948; 7 September 1956).

———. "Church of the Open Door." Sermon preached at First Baptist Church of Dallas, 9 June 1968.

———. *Criswell's Guidebook for Pastors.* Nashville: Broadman, 1980.

———. *Ecclesiology.* Vol. 3 of *Great Doctrines of the Bible.* Grand Rapids: Zondervan, 1983.

———. "Walking by Faith Alone." Sermon preached at First Baptist Church of Dallas, 31 August 1986.

________. "Our Prayer Answering God." Sermon preached at First Baptist Church of Dallas, 3 December 1986.

________. "Founder's Day Message." Sermon preached at First Baptist Church of Dallas, 29 September 1987.

________. Review of *The Southern Baptist Holy War*, by Joe Edward Barnhart. *Criswell Theological Review* 3:453-56.

________. "The Fifth Commandment." Sermon preached at First Baptist Church of Dallas, 5 May 1988.

DuCasse, R. *A History of the First Baptist Church, Dallas, Texas*. Master's thesis. Dallas Theological Seminary, 1964.

Jennings, D. "High Profile: W. A. Criswell." *Dallas Morning News*, 1 December 1985.

Keith, B. *W. A. Criswell: The Authorized Biography*. Old Tappan, N.J.: Revell, 1973.

McBeth, Leon. *The First Baptist Church of Dallas*. Grand Rapids: Zondervan, 1968.

Patterson, Paige."The Imponderables of God." *Criswell Theological Review* 1:237-53.

Reavis, Dick. "The Politics of Armageddon." *Texas Monthly* (October 1984): 162-66, 235-46.

Roberts, C. M. *W. A. Criswell's Choice and Use of Illustrations*. Master's thesis. Dallas Theological Seminary, 1976.

Russell, C. Allyn. *Voices of American Fundamentalism: Seven Biographical Studies*. Philadelphia: Westminster, 1976.

Taylor, M., ed. *Changing Patterns of Religious Education*. Nashville: Abingdon, 1984.

Towns, J. E. *The Rhetoric and Leadership of W. A. Criswell as President of the Southern Baptist Conven-*

tion: A Descriptive Analysis Through Perspective and Public Address. Doctoral diss. Southern Illinois University, 1970.

________. *The Social Conscience of W. A. Criswell.* Dallas: Crescendo, 1977.

Moody Press, a ministry of Moody Bible Institute,
is designed for education, evangelization, and edification.
If we may assist you in knowing more about Christ
and the Christian life, please write us without obligation:
Moody Press, c/o MLM, Chicago, Illinois 60610.